AF490666

A Long Look Back

A Sentimental Journey of an American Growing Up in France

RICHARD H. ROGERS

Copyright © 2022 Richard H Rogers

All rights reserved. No part of this book may be reproduced or transmitted in form or by any means, electronic or mechanical, including photocopying, recording, or by any information storage and retrieval system without the permission of the publisher, except in the case of brief quotations embodied in critical reviews and articles.

This book is dedicated to my dear children and grandchildren.

Table of Contents

Introduction   ix

PART I: MADE IN BRITTANY – THE EMERALD COAST   1

The Country Mailman: *Monsieur le Facteur*   3

A House in Brittany – *Une Maison en Bretagne*   7

Laddie's Corner: Saying our Last Goodbyes to
Man's Best Friend   15

Of Holidays and *Réveillons* Past   19

A Rabbit's Tale: *Lapin à la Moutarde en Cocotte*   22

A Country Walk   24

That Summer Vacation Long Ago   31

On Vacation: Roasted Chicken with Lemon and Rosemary
or *En Vacance: Poulet Rôti au Citron et au Romarin*   37

Coastal West France: An Atlantic Culinary Trilogy   39

Part 1: The Adventure Begins: *Le Touquet, Deauville
et Dinard*   39

Part 2: The Adventure Continues: *Cape Ferret,
Biarritz et Saint Jean de Luz*   55

More (Modern Day) Memories Made in Brittany   73

Mussels in White Wine: *Moules Marinières* 79

Leg of Lamb, Brittany-Style: *Gigot d'Agneau à
     la Bretonne* 82

Best French Comfort Foods: Settling in for the Winter 84

Gratineed Chicken in Cream Sauce: *Poulet à la Fermière* 87

World Famous Bicycle Race Comes Home 89

A Long Weekend in Brittany 100

PART II: MADE IN PARIS 123

Growing up in Paris: Background 125

Le Jardin des Tuileries: Master and Commander 130

A Snapshot of our Neuilly-sur-Seine 133

The American Cathedral on Avenue George V 137

A Most Remarkable Person 143

Isadora Duncan and the Last Social Season in Paris 148

The Vice Consul or A Secret Exchange in *Auteuil* 151

A Passing Glimpse of Paris, circa 1926 161

Snapshots of Growing Up in Neuilly-sur-Seine 164

Alumni Daze or My Personal *Rentrée Scolaire* (the
     start of the school year) 183

A French Butcher May be the Nearest Thing to God 189

In Defense of Good Manners: *La Politesse Avant Tout* 191

We Have Examined Your Dossier, Monsieur 193

Ms. Edith's Travel Agency: French Dreams for Sale 198

The House at Twelve Ginger Lane: From Beijing to Paris:
     From Chopsticks to Croissants 204

Falling In Love in Clichy 209

Thanksgiving Dinner in Liberated Paris 213

The Last Breakfast in Paris   217
Why I Left Paris (Because Things Inevitably Get
    Complicated)   221

PART III: TOWARDS THE COTE D'AZUR   231
A Tasty *Bouchon* Lyonnais   233
Diner in the Garden of France
    (Fricassée de Volaille au Vouvray)   237
A Memorable Dinner in *Languedoc-Roussillon*   240
Black Truffle Hunting I Go   247
Breakfast in Vieux Nice at *Le Coin Quotidien*   253
Lunch in Vieux Nice at *Bistro d'Antoine*   256
Le Cannet, the Chocolate Festival and Room for Dinner   259
Seafood Risotto Dinner on the rue *Masséna* in Nice   264
Hors-Season – Antibes/Juan Les Pins   267
Back to the Wine Futures   272
Swordfish Niçoise – *Espadon à la Niçoise*   276

PART IV: SELECTED RECIPES   279
Roasted Chicken with Lemon and Rosemary   280
Chicken with Onions, Calvados, and Cream   282
Pan-Fried Steaks with Mustard Cream Sauce   285
Rabbit in Mustard Sauce   287
Seared Scallops with Tarragon-Butter Sauce   289
Poulet à la Normande   291
Gratineed Chicken in Cream Sauce   293
Swordfish Niçoise; *Espadon à la Niçoise*   295
Fricassée of Chicken with Vouvray Wine   297

Sautéed Pork Chops in Green Peppercorn
    Mustard Cream Sauce   299
Pork Chops in a Green Peppercorn Mustard Sauce   300
Tuna Basque-style: *Thon à la Basquaise*   302

About The Author   305

INTRODUCTION

Creating this book has been a labor of love for me and now it is my turn to share my passion with you. The book has three distinct sections: Brittany, Paris/Neuilly, and the South of France. I have also included a separate chapter devoted to mouth-watering recipes I know you will want to try out for yourself and I would urge you do so. Of course with a little wine, just to be safe. How can anyone fully appreciate France without its mouth-watering cuisine? I authored this book as a memoir of my childhood years in Paris and wonderful summers spent with my family in Brittany. This collection of stories is a look back at those rich years in France. It is undeniably a wonderful and sentimental and sentimental journey in a country so dear to my heart.

If you are a foodie you will love some of my stories. You will be joining me on a wonderful six-part culinary trip along France's Atlantic Coast and visiting wonderful locations that are as grand now as they were a hundred years ago or more. We start with a visit to the Opal Coast and the well-known resort of *Le Touquet*, where my father spent his youthful summers in the late 1920s. Then join me for an unforgettable dinner in Dinard, a popular holiday destination in Brittany set in the beautiful and deeply familiar *Côte d' Émeraude*. Finally, we finish our journey in the unique and picturesque seaport town of Saint-Jean-de Luz, nestled in Basque country. It is a journey stuffed with deliciously rich and creamy memorable local experiences. The food, the wine, and the richness of these beautiful locations are unbeatable. All of which will surely have you packing your bags and heading to France in no time!

The first part of the book includes a number of stories that take place in Brittany, many will surely appeal to your foodie senses. This western region of France, Brittany, has played a major part in my life, both as a child when we bought the house then as an adult. My memories of family vacations in the early days are vivid. Rough, crude flooring, stained pink-wash walls, an ever-malfunctioning fireplace leaving us in tears from the smoke, a dampness that abounded, a small bottled gas stove, more suitable for camping than in a kitchen, no refrigerator as one was not really needed and an of course there was the outhouse in the back garden. As children we would go to bed with multiple blankets and armed with a hot water bottle to ward off the chill from the damp sheets. We were pioneers. My father failed to understand why we were less than excited as the at the prospect of the family spending Christmas in Brittany. Many of the stories were inspired by those days at the country house and provided me with a richness of content for many of my stories. Additionally, I have tried to convey our rural, rugged Brittany, which at that time, had not significantly changed since the 1940's.

In part two, I recount my childhood growing up in Paris, the leafy suburbs of Neuilly-sur-Seine, a stone's throw from the Paris city limits and the 16e arrondissement where my brothers and I attended school. We lived in a newly built, spacious apartment and we had all the room necessary to stir-up trouble. Paris in the late 1950's and early 1960s had the Algerian conflict as a backdrop. The OAS were planting bombs in theaters and cafes across France.

The trials and tribulations of a young American, and particularly my challenges in surviving the French school system are a part of my story. I never really "got it" despite the French educational system's best efforts to turn me into a good *citoyen*, at whatever cost to me or the mental anguish. I was more than relieved having to leave school and I retained, for many years, a deep sense of personal discomfort well into my adult life.

Many years later, returning to France on a business trip to Paris, I recount having a most memorable dinner at the *Café Bergamote* a cozy little resto' nestled on the Left Bank at 8, *rue Montfaucon* in the sixth *arrondisement*. What a spectacular dinner and you will be joining me there.

In part three, I take a leisurely journey towards the coast, eventually reaching the beautiful Mediterranean. Join me at "*Chez M'man*" for a memorable first stop at a tasty *Bouchon Lyonnais*, if ever there was one, and located near the charming *Place Bellecour* on the *rue des Maronniers*. One cannot help falling in love with Lyon, over and over again. A beautiful city that is often called the culinary capital of France and the gastronomic capital of the world. Yes, the food is beyond superb, fantastic restaurants and incredible chefs. What fun to stop on your way home and watch the young chefs in culinary school busy in the kitchen! Typical foods on the menu in this *Bouchon* includes such local specialties as andouille (grilled chitterlings sausage), tripe (pig or cow's stomach), or *boudin noir* (blood sausage). Other, perhaps, more recognizable dishes include, chicken liver salad, *Cerverlas,* (raw pork sausages), *Quenelles* (flour, egg, and cream dumplings.) May I suggest, to add to your dining pleasure, one or two wonderful Beaujolais? Moving southward, I recount a memorable dinner at a little restaurant tucked away in the 12th Century fortified village of Rivesaltes in the Languedoc Roussillon region. A truly spectacular and memorable meal.

MADE IN BRITTANY – THE EMERALD COAST

The Country Mailman: Monsieur le Facteur

I genuinely believe that nothing is more sacred in France than the lunch hour. Whether you are sitting in a busy café in Paris, in a bathing suit at a *station balnéaire* or summer resort, or just relaxing quietly out in the country somewhere, checkered tablecloth and all. It's all the same. To miss out on lunch well, it's like missing out on life. And it is just not done.

At the old family house in Brittany, we would be having lunch, all of us as a family, sitting around the large dining room table, the shutters, and windows all open, and the curtains swaying ever so gently from an occasional ocean summer breeze. This time of day, it was quiet outside, even cars usually packed with tourists on summer outing had found a little place to stop for lunch. Yes, it was a sacred moment in the day. People stopped what they were doing, gathered around and broke bread. Well, almost all.

We had just finished soaking up the last of a delicious vinaigrette, with beautiful home-grown tomatoes and having made sure to carefully wipe with a piece of bread every square inch of our plates so not to miss even a drop. Without a warning the bell on the front gate jingled as it was being pushed open by a man of some size with a large leather bag strapped around his chest, and his official hat tilted back on his head revealing beads of perspiration. The French state never sleeps.

Simone, our dear housekeeper, three-star Michelin cook, confidant, country doctor and timely bearer of all the bad news that *Ouest France* could publish, greeted *Monsieur le Facteur*. Country pleasantries and local gossip were exchanged as both were, *du pays*. And, as if on cue, my father turned around and ask *Monsieur le Facteur* if he would care to join us for a little glass of red wine, *un petit verre de vin Monsieur?* It is good business to be polite in these parts. Pedaling a bicycle with his bulging mailbag around country roads all day can give a man powerful thirst. How could he say no to such a kind offer?

The second course was quietly kept on hold while this little ritual played itself out.

There we were all nursing our wine or in my case watered-down wine (the injustice of it all), my parents making small talk about the weather (warm for this early in the season), the unusual amount of tourists (seems like more than ever this year), the markets (hard to find that special something) and *Monsieur le Facteur* also doing his share to carry on the conversation in a very heavy Breton *patoit* or local accent.

A second round was offered but respectfully declined by *Monsieur le Facteur* who then collected his bicycle and walked out the gate. Until the next time when a letter or a postcard would be delivered. I don't know if any of us every knew his name or why we should have. As far as we knew he was always *Monsieur le Facteur*. That was it.

At long last, the second course was presented, and Simone would place it in front of my father, with much flourish and a corresponding "*ooo—la-la*" on our part. This time the *piece de resistance* was a *colin en sauce blanche* (hake fish) with its head still firmly attached and smothered in a delicious cream sauce with capers and boiled potatoes from our vegetable garden. The *colin* and I had a staring contest going on and I believe I may have blinked first. When the *colin* was a mere bony shadow of its former self, dinner plates were removed and replaced with a third round for the cheeses and a tossed green salad fresh from the vegetable garden, of course. More bread and more wine if you please. Finally, it was desert time and a special one had been prepared just for Simone's favorite *petit chou-chou* (OK, that would be me folks). The *crepes* were proudly presented table-side, and we added sugar or jam or both, if no one was looking. My father would abstain and state unequivocally: "I can't see how you could possibly eat that sweet stuff after such a delicious meal." Finally, with our additional poundage, we made our way outside for coffee. This meant we could look forward to having a "*canne a sucre*" or a sugar cube that was dipped in coffee.

Our stomachs now completely full and our system properly sugared, it was time to consider the options. Maybe some light reading in the deck chair out in the garden, perhaps a nap upstairs, or was I going to be shanghaied into making yet another trip with my father and my brothers to an antique store, another *magasin de brochante*. Please God, no.

That luncheon scene was typical of the many meals we had while gathered around the table on those lovely, slow summer days in Brittany. We ate like kings, we swam in the ocean like fish and played with an old patched-up yellow WWII-era Navy rubber raft that my father had found somewhere, we took long walk to nowhere, and played like the kids we were in a summer we felt certain would last forever.

When I returned many years later, as an adult, I opened wide the dining room windows onto the courtyard and enjoyed the late afternoon breeze as it gently moved the curtains and filled the room with that beautiful fresh country air. There I sat at the same dining room table and in the same ladder-back chairs I use to complain about as a young boy as cruel punishment. I listened quietly, letting my mind and my senses travel back once more to those days now long gone. The same smells, the loud ticking of the grandfather clock, the sound of feet running upstairs then scrambling down the well-worn staircase, the occasional sound of a car zipping by on its way to the beach or the lighthouse at the Cap Frehel. What I was visualizing was as clear as a bell for me, and I know I heard our Simone call out *tout le monde at table*! Sit down everyone, it's time for lunch! Memories last. They most certainly do.

A House in Brittany – *Une Maison en Bretagne*

More than just a few years ago, my older brothers, my two sisters and I were fortunate enough to have spent many a summer at our family's summer home, wisely purchased by my father in the late 1950s and located in a small village in Brittany, a mere bike ride to that beautiful emerald coastline.

Prior to our arrival, the only other Americans who had visited the village came in a jeep and a tank in the summer of 1944.

August 15, 1944, American soldiers liberate our little village in Brittany

I can still vividly recall those summer mornings when we would wake up to the sounds of cow bells ringing, signaling that the farmer from across the street was herding his cows up the road and into the pasture next to our house. What little traffic there was, a *camionette*, would stop and patiently wait for the cows to move along. We boys would push open the shutters flat out against the side of the house and get our first glimpse of the glorious summer day, full of possibilities. Many years later, I recalled how pleased I was that my grown children and daughter in law also had a chance to enjoy our home and even see the farmer (now the son, who I knew from growing up next door) herding his cows and my children even had a chance to milk them. A wonderful part of country life, yet I suspect, as far removed as anything from their urban life back home in the United States.

From the very beginning, the house was my father's a passion. He was determined in his desire to turn an old 1890s *Maison de Maître* into a nice, livable country home. Granted, when he purchased it, it was about as far from that dream as anyone could have imagined. Inside, I can recall, all too clearly, that it was cold and very damp. It had uneven, rough earthen floors, a large, stained fireplace that refused to draw well so it was smoky and left my poor mother perpetually in tears. I can recall coming downstairs for breakfast wrapped in sweaters and there was mother herself wrapped up trying with one hand to negotiate a recalcitrant fireplace and the other negotiating a toaster, the kind that opened on both sides. It was smoky blue.

Elsewhere, the walls were stained a pale pink wash and we had only the very rudimentary necessities including an old propane stove, no shower, nor tub and one temperamental toilet and tiny bathroom sink. But there was an outhouse in the back yard, and I remember fumbling my way in the dark to find it! We are not talking about a weekend warrior's little fixer-upper, far from it! At the time of the purchase, it was the late 1950's in very rural France. My father saw no reason for not wanting to spend the upcoming holidays at the house. It would be so much fun he insisted. I don't recall a smile on anyone's face. Somehow hopping into an ice-cold, damp four-poster bed armed with only a sweater and a hot water bottle and a good book to read challenged all of us to be sure.

My father, in the slow process of renovation, would spend endless hours hunting down someone in the village or the neighboring one, who could repair or knew someone who could repair an antiquated stove, or an electrician who could find the right fuses for the fuse box, a roofer to replace missing slate roof shingles, a plumber who could install something resembling a heating system, or perhaps someone who could clean out the fireplace before we kids burned the house to the ground. At that time, there was no project management software to bring up on an iPad, there was not even a phone in the house although we were on the list, but it would take several years before anything happened. For my father, the challenges must have seemed endless. On more than one occasion I accompanied my brothers on these trips to neighboring towns with my father determined to strike a deal with the local electrician, plumber, or other tradesman. I must admit, my father was quite good at it. Once a business deal was struck and promises were made for a date certain, it was only the beginning of my father's headaches.

The concept of time takes on a entirely different meaning in the country. I honestly believe this, and I also believe my father came to realize that himself, although perhaps grudgingly at first. My father, pleased with himself for having locked in several tradesmen for jobs meant that he was now acting as general contractor/babysitter/taskmaster and had to remind each one when they were expected to appear on such and such day and time. Follow-up without a phone made things just a little more challenging and all the more frustrating for someone like my father who got easily frustrated. Playing cat and mouse was not his sport. Back and forth we went to neighboring towns and villages reminding the carpenter or the plumber of their appointment only to learn from their wives that someone would not be there until the following-week for any number of reasons. They needed to find parts in another town, there was a death in the family, they were not feeling well, a christening, a hangover and on and on. Then one day, usually around breakfast time, when my father, still in his dressing gown, having his coffee and stewing over the state of things, there would be a knock at the door, and there stood the electrician or the plumber who been missing in action and late by one or two weeks or more. No excuses given.

Work would have to start in the kitchen or somewhere it did not matter, but the tradesmen quickly assured my father that he could always come back if it were more convenient. Simone, our dear housekeeper, and fabulous cook more often than not knew the tradesmen, and they would spend a fair amount of time chatting about local town gossip and of course, always the latest dreadful car accidents on some local road, a tourist falling off a cliff, a child run over by a speeding tourist, one story after another. Who needed a newspaper? This was better than *Ouest France.* At the end of the day, the plumber or someone else would pick up their tools, load up their truck with a sworn promise to my father that they would return in two days to finish the job. Two days, in country time, would invariably stretch into a week or more or until we paid him a personal visit or reminded his wife. That seemed to usually work, in most cases. This scenario would repeat itself time and time again over a period of many years.

In my adult years, returning to Brittany was for me always tremendously nostalgic. Thomas Wolfe, the great American author noted that *"Some things will never change. Some things will always be the same. Lean down your ear upon the earth and listen."*

On returning to France one year, I made the trip back to the old homestead. I learned that our dear housekeeper was still with us, and at that time, she was, I suspect, in her early nineties. I decided I had to pay her visit but only after having first arranged it with her husband who I had met walking down a country lane, both of us clearly enjoying the weather. There he was with his beret, rough working clothes, ever-ruddy complexion and always a shy smile. We were clearly both happy to see each other. The last time I had seen Simone I was 21 years old. so, a considerable amount of time, more than twenty years, had passed. As I walked up the little lane to her home, I saw her there sitting on the bench, enjoying the remains of the day, the warm late afternoon September sun as she waited patiently for my arrival. What a joyful reunion it was! We hugged each other warmly after so many years it was a wonderful bittersweet reunion that has been seared in my memory. Her tears of joy ran down her weathered, wrinkled beautiful, sweet face. I still get emotional when I think about that moment and as I write about it. She was, in many ways, and I will repeat it once more, almost like a surrogate mother to me.

Simone, would tolerate me in the kitchen and I remember shadowing her movements, cleaning up this or that, chopping up one thing or another and most importantly, learning how to get out of her way at critical moments in the cooking process. Of course, witnessing a duck or rabbit's immediate and definite demise was always part of the deal

With remarkable ease, I found myself slipping back in time and space. I did not walk up the steps I bounded up the wooden stairs running to my room as if I was thirteen years old. Downstairs I opened the French doors and eagerly stepped out into the front courtyard and started walking the property. Were those the same cows in the field? I exchanged a friendly wave with the farmer as he drove by on his tractor; we were both kids many years ago. How things appeared not to have really changed. Maybe the *potage*r or vegetable garden looked smaller, there in the far corner we buried are dear cocker spaniel. There was a time when the *potager* had been filled with lettuce, potatoes, leeks, string beans, radishes, and much more. The delicate little pear trees on either side of the garden path still survived these many years and those tart cooking apples fallen from the old tree were there once again lying on the grass waiting for me. I threw one out into the field somewhere because I was somewhere else in another time. The majestic old fig tree still overshadowed the courtyard and seemed even larger than before. A few figs on the ground waited to be picked up or maybe thrown at the enemy hiding behind the farmer's fence. A major fig battle of yesteryear with the farmers kids might soon erupt.

A quick word about the term "comfort food" which in France is known as "*Cuisine Grand-Mère*" or Grand Mother's (i.e., comfort food) cooking. All things being equal, I think that's an appropriate name. For me, this type of cooking conjures up a special image of a friendly, ruddy-faced country woman with coal black eyes and a quick smile, wearing a blue and white checked apron and decked-out in country slippers or a pair of *sabots* or clogs. It also makes me think of someone who could prepare the most incredibly delicious country meals on the one hand, and on the other perfectly

I learned a fair share about French country food, its history and preparation as well as one or two country tall tales. The Bretons are a mystical people in many ways and all one has to do is read the Arthurian tales and visit or explore the *foret de Brocéliande.*

The story goes on as it must. Brittany is as beautiful a place as it ever was and ever will be. The warm summer and the Fall are idyllic to me. What is equally fascinating is that I am able to return to the old place, and I know it will feel to me as if I have reached my family's ground zero, in a sense. To be honest, I have never felt as close to my parent's spirit as when I am in Brittany. Not Paris, Antwerp, Brussels, the Congo, or even the USA. So much passion, energy, and emotions have camped in that house, for better or for worse. I can feel it and it's all good.

Laddie's Corner: Saying our Last Goodbyes to Man's Best Friend

View of the small courtyard leading to the garden.

I believe few things can be as traumatic in a young boy's life as the passing of a much beloved family dog. And so it was for me.

We sat on the outside steps to the courtyard, my brothers and I, awaiting the return of our Cocker Spaniel Laddie. On that late summer afternoon, when things stand still and quiet, I suspect we were all somewhere lost in our own thoughts. I know I was. The low buzz of a passing bumblebee, an occasional breeze drifting from the sea would gently rustle the leaves of the old fig tree that held a commanding presence in the courtyard. Somewhere off in the distance, the sound of a bicycle bell ringing as a lone rider made his way down to the village. In the fields adjacent to our home, a cow occasionally reminded us of its presence. We waited some more. The grandfather clock momentarily shattered the silence and struck the hours solemnly, as if it too, were in pain. Then quiet again. A fig dropped with a sound as it hit the graveled courtyard and lay there momentarily before one of my brothers picked it up and threw it high over the gate and across the road to the farm. A well-placed shot was always a good thing as the fig wars may have stopped for a while, they certainly did not signal a total cessation of war.

Sitting on the steps, we said nothing and watched nothing in particular. Then we heard the unmistakable sound of the Peugeot horn. The sound could just as well have been an air raid horn going off, warning us to take cover but it was too late. My father was signaling us to open the gates so that he could drive into the courtyard. I watched as the Peugeot rumbled to a stop beneath the old fig tree. That moment I had hoped would never arrive yet knowing somehow in my heart it would inevitably come, was finally here. I dreaded it and felt sick to my stomach. My father, in a white button-down shirt, long khaki pants and loafers stepped out of the car and gave us all a look that needed no explanation. He felt as bad as we all did, and I felt myself biting my lower lip to stop it from trembling and valiantly attempting to hold back my tears. How unfair was this? It was not supposed to happen, never, ever. As the trunk was unlocked and opened, we three boys cautiously peered in only to see a rug which we knew held Laddie's last remains.

"Come on boys, give me hand, each of you take a corner of the rug and I'll get the shovel."

My father led the procession, shovel in hand, then came my brothers each holding a side of the rug with Laddie, and I following behind. Perhaps the only thing missing was a top hat on my father's head, me twirling an umbrella high in the air and the sounds of a New Orleans funeral dirge playing in the background. Slowly we proceeded from the courtyard pass the little white garden gate and into the garden. We walked slowly and the only sound were our footsteps crunching along the graveled path, passing the pear and apple trees and finally through the last gate and stopping at the far-right hand corner of the *potager* or vegetable garden, Laddie's designated final resting place. He would go no further ever again. My brothers took turns digging a deep hole, my father smoked a Kent cigarette looking at nothing in particular, emotions had passed, and some things just had to be done that was that. I do not know what I expected him to say or for that matter, do. It felt like an out of body experience, me watching myself watching the burial. The rug was unfolded, and I caught my last look at Laddie, his black and white coat, his grey muzzle, and his eyes closed, forever. Into the hole he was placed but without the rug which had been unceremoniously rescued by my father "it's still a perfectly decent rug, no use throwing it away." After many shovelfuls later it was all over. Just like that, the end. We were left with our memories of Laddie; memories which would inevitably fade forever, or perhaps not entirely.

Many years later when I finally returned for a long stay at the family home in Brittany, I found myself strolling down to the old *potager,* swing open the gate and walk back to Laddie's corner and remember. I will do it again next time. I hope he understands.

OF HOLIDAYS AND *RÉVEILLONS PAST*

Several years ago, and I must add, by some stroke of good fortune we all managed to find our way back to the family home in France, tucked away in a remote little village, a bike ride away from the rugged but ever so beautiful Brittany coast. It had been a complex and coordinated logistical feat to make it happen and I am positive it rivaled preparations for the D-Day invasion. We had all gathered in this special place to celebrate the holidays, together.

Once in France, I rented a little Peugeot just large enough for a European family of four, two bicycles, a dog, and a cat or one American and a suitcase. I stuffed myself behind the wheel and shot out of the station like a slingshot, a horse out of the starting gate or a dog who knew his way home and no one was going to stop him.

Before I knew it, I was off the *Route Nationale* and taking a short cut which put me on familiar winding country roads. The sky was a majestic blue, everything smelled rich and delicious, and the country air went through me like a welcomed guest; it was pure and invigorating air and made you feel glad just to be alive! I drove along the coast road, windows down, breathing in that familiar tangy smell of low tide, and navigating more hairpin turns on narrow one lane roads. Finally, I knew I was but a few hundred yards from the family home. Turning into the graveled driveway, the race was over, I was home.

Returning to France my birthplace and Brittany, the family home in particular is always tremendously nostalgic. And with good reason. My family has been associated with France off and on since 1913. My father purchased the old property circa late 1890's in the summer of 1959. As kids we spent many a summer there as my father determinedly brought the house up to his ship-shape standards and we all never ceased to enjoy one feast after another.

Our New Year's Eve dinner was as simple as it was elegant. We started with mussels in white wine. The mussels were courtesy of Monsieur Julien from across the street. He and his wife had a thriving seafood "side business" that is run out of the back of their garage and no one's the wiser and lest of all the tax man. We would often get our mussels there and feast on them, Madame reminded us: *un kilo par personne monsieur*! (Three kilograms per person if you are not having them as your principal meal.)

A local *foie gras* (goose liver) *en croûte de pain d'épices* would be offered and there were cases of wine and champagne courtesy of the Super U's finest selection of spirits, and all stacked neatly outside the kitchen door just waiting to be introduced. We all had a mighty thirst. More Champagne please!

The diner's center piece was a *Gigot d'agneau à la Bretonne* or a Leg of Lamb Brittany-Style. It tastes the same either way and courtesy to *monsieur le boucher,* the butcher, down the street. A beautiful tossed salad and a selection of cheeses and of course for dessert the very traditional *Bûche de Noël* or Yule Log, which had been ordered well ahead of time from the only *boulangerie* in the village. With the spectacular desert came a super-sized box of Godiva chocolates and Cognac (both grabbed by yours' truly at the duty-free shop), liqueurs and a fine selection of *eau de vie, Poire* being my special favorite.

It was a memorable meal that evening and magical in so many ways. As the candles slowly melted down, we talked ourselves hoarse about everything and everyone, past and present, good times and sad. Champagne, wine, and brandy seemed to flow forever. Re-united *en-famille* everyone sensed the power and meaning of this special moment and wanting it to last forever.

The gears on the old Grandfather clock slowly wound up then solemnly and deeply chimed once, then twice finally reaching twelve midnight. Glasses were raised to welcome the new year. It was a single, magical moment in time. From somewhere in village the popping sounds of fireworks could be heard as they made their way up into an incredibly clear and starry *Breton* midnight sky.

A Rabbit's Tale: *Lapin à la Moutarde en Cocotte*

These are times when I find more rabbit dishes to seriously contemplate than there are rabbits. Rabbit stew inevitably takes me back to those days when, as a child, we would spend our holidays, *en famille*, at the house tucked away in the Brittany countryside. It was quite cold (chilly and damp perhaps but typical for Brittany) but when our dear cook announced that she was making her famous rabbit dish that news guaranteed to warm us up.

I will spare you the details of the early morning execution of said "wabbit" other than mentioning, for the record, that he did not stand a hare's chance of ever being proven innocent. To the sound of a slow drumbeat, rascal wabbit was un-ceremoniously marched down the gravel path from the kitchen back door to the garden and from there, ten paces to ye old apple tree. He was offered his last *Gauloise* cigarette or was it a carrot from our potager? I don't recall. He was then tied to a large branch. Our country cook's weapon of choice was a long, menacing, razor sharp kitchen knife with a well-worn handle. The deed was swift and surgically perfect and I, ever the lucky one, was offered a now limp, still draining rabbit to carry back to the kitchen. Country living at its finest.

I found the rabbit recipe just in time for a New Year's Eve dinner I was preparing and even found a butcher in town who promised he would have one ready and he did not skin me alive, either. The meal was a spectacular success, and I chose an exceptional wine from the southern Rhone valley, *Chateau Pesquie Terrasses*. It was a no brainer selection after all what better than a wine from the part of the country where people live long comfortable lives in the sun in a region where most rabbit days are numbered.

A Country Walk

It was a brilliant blue sky the likes of which he had not seen in a long time. From somewhere off in the distance, he heard his father's booming voice hurrying him home for the noon meal and then he heard his brothers running past betting who would get home first. He knew his mother would be waiting at the door and wondering. He could see her now, her hands on her hips and finger wagging side to side, trying hard to keep a serious face for her little favorite. The sharp pains in his chest seemed to ease for a moment. He felt tired, deeply tired. He just wanted to rest for a little while longer. He closed his eyes. He would be home soon. He promised himself.

A late Fall afternoon in the Brittany countryside can be beautiful to behold. The sky is quite often painted a majestic bright blue with just a few well-placed clouds and when combined with a gentle off-shore breeze, everything was about as near-perfect as one could have wanted. The back country roads for the most part were quiet, absent the usual whine of tourists motoring furiously towards the village before the bakery closed for the noon hour or perhaps driving the back roads to the beach past house after house, each tucked well away from prying eyes and most with their shutters long closed for the season. Late Fall, away from the urbanized regions, the pace around these parts slows down considerably and one is more likely to come across a herd of cows than a herd of tourists.

According to the church bells which seemed to mark the passage of time in these parts, it was already past noon and gates were closed, front doors were shut and most families were indoors seated, *a table,* enjoying their big meal of the day. However, not for Madame Armelle Fourchon, the farmer's wife who waited patiently seated in her spotlessly clean kitchen, her rough hands that spoke volumes of life on the farm, were folded and resting on the simple plastic tablecloth. Their fancy new wall clock, weather barometer combination and made in Germany, announced it was half-past the noon hour. She had never known her husband, Alphonse to ever be late this late for the noonday meal. Not ever. He was most likely having a lively discussion about new farm machinery, government ineptness, elections, and general village gossip. Most likely all this over a few *apero's.*

It was Bernard, the local *Garde Champetre* the one responsible for keeping poachers at bay, who found him sitting there in his family field, leaning peacefully his back against one of the poplar trees that had all been neatly planted in a row marking the end of his property and the beginning of his neighbors. As he crossed the field, Bernard called out Fourchon's name once, then again wondering to himself what was his brother-in-law doing there rather than seated at the lunch table with his wife who just happened to be Bernard's oldest sister. Fourchon lay there, quite still, his coarse flannel shirt unbuttoned midway revealing a stained undershirt and a St. Christopher medallion that gleamed as it caught the early afternoon sun. Clutching his blue beret in his lap, he lay there half seated, half lying and wearing on his face a befuddled, almost questioning look.

Monsieur Alphonse Fourchon, the last of ten children, had passed away, that much Bernard knew at least from his training with the *sapeurs-pompiers volontaires* and the *service mobile d'urgence,* the volunteer fire department and the local rescue squad. Useful training, yes indeed but just a tad too late to do any good to ol' Fourchon, his now very much deceased brother-in-law. He would tell his sister immediately then call the authorities, of course. There would be *une enquete* an investigation of some sort he thought to himself, as a matter of formality.

That Monsieur Alphonse Fourchon was advancing in years was an indisputable fact but obtaining any hard empirical evidence to support that indisputable fact was a horse of an entirely different color. With his ruddy complexion, shock of white hair and jet-black eyes typical *du pays,* he was a well-known site in the village. For sure, his normal impatient hurried walk was a little slower, but he still managed to show his eldest son, Jean-Marie the proper way, which would be his way, of herding the cows to and from the barn early each morning and in the evening followed by the milking process. Madame Armelle Fourchon, black-eyes, black curly hair streaked with grey and an equally ruddy complexion, tolerated at best her husband's insistence that he be allowed to drive the old red tractor at harvest time however she clearly and quite firmly put her foot down when it came to any notion that he could climb up and into the monstrous *moissonneuse batteuse* or combine harvester and then attempt to drive. No that was not going to happen as long as she was standing. The harvester was as least as tall as a two or maybe even a three-story building and looked as if it might have once been used to destroy heavily fortified positions in another era; the enemy would have most surely turned and run at the sight of a green and red monster approaching, lights flashing, sharp red teeth tearing up, chewing, and spitting out everything in its path. If you were unlucky enough to find yourself driving behind the harvester and driver on his way to the fields, you settled in for a long, slow ride. One reached their destination eventually. Country life.

Alphonse Fourchon had always been a farmer just like his father *Vieux* Fourchon or "old man Fourchon." According to the village gossip, you could set your clock by *le vieux*. If you saw him dressed in his finest shirt and pants walking down the street holding flowers, it was most likely a Wednesday and just past eleven o'clock and old man Fourchon was paying his respects to his parents at the cemetery the way he had been doing every week for so many years he had forgotten just how many. Traditions die hard in the country if they ever died at all. Alphonse, also known as *le jeune Fourchon*, young Fourchon even though he was close to seventy years old had continued on the family habit of paying his respects.

It was Wednesday morning and by the looks of the bright blue sky, it was going to be a beautiful day. Madame was, in a tender moment, making sure Alphonse was ready for his walk down to the cemetery. She buttoned the top button then gently smoothed down his well-worn flannel shirt. She inspected his blue working man's pants and despite the season of the year, Alphonse knew she would always say, "now it's chilly outside, so make sure you button your sweater and keep your beret on dear. This time don't stay too long after you paid your respects." She knew her husband would think about stopping at the *Bar-Tabac* on his way home in event he might catch one of his of *copains* or friends. There was always the distinct possibility of having a little glass of something before lunch. The infamous *"petit verre."*

With flowers in hand, grey sweater vest buttoned up and his beret firmly atop his head, Monsieur Alphonse Fourchon walked out the front door of their immaculate little house, swung opened the little gate but making sure to hook it closed after him, turned right and slowly began his walk alongside the road to the *Cimetière du village* or the village cemetery. It could be a challenging walk while in full tourist season as car after car would speed by him in a blur. Today, only one car speed past him, a gleaming blue, two-door, Peugeot with the tale-tale "75" on the license plate. A Parisian around these parts, especially after the season was rare. Speeding however was always in season.

As country cemeteries go, it would hardly stand out as anything truly spectacular if in fact cemeteries can ever be, but it was, nevertheless, the final resting place for generations of village locals. There were a few oddities or items of interest if one took the time to stroll about. There was the grave of a Canadian fly boy, deceased June 1944, undoubtedly shot down by German anti-aircraft that would have dotted the coast as part of the Atlantic wall defenses; there was an elegant tombstone of a Baron of some uncertain nationality, who died apparently from a duel gone bad in 1911, and just steps away, a child of just a few years resting there since 1942. Two rows over from the Canadian, Alphonse stopped and took of his beret in respect, arranged the flowers as best he could for *Maman et Papa*. He spoke softly, your son is doing fine and, yes, he missed you both very much. That was done.

Leaving the cemetery, Alphonse could have turned right and retraced his steps home, but he thought perhaps his friend Hervé might be standing at the counter of the Bar-Tabac, having a coffee with a little Cognac and a pack of forbidden *Gauloise* cigarettes safely by his side. In short, everything the doctor had warned him about and reminded daily by his wife. Hervé was sure he had cancer brought on by an incessant tobacco habit combined with the accumulated quarry dust that had settled in his lungs for the duration. He had spent most of his adult life working the quarry on the outskirts of town near the salt marshes and the infrequent high tides. It was hard, back-breaking work but it was all he had ever done and it's what he did best.

There he was leaning against the bar chatting up the young *serveuse* or bartender just as Alphonse had figured.

"*Bonjour Alphonse*" she chirped seeing him come in. "*Un Ricard, comme d'habitude ?*"

The milky, anisette flavored drink went down a little too fast. It had a habit of doing so. Yes, another please. Hervé pointed a nicotine-stained index finder in the direction of the racing forms.

"This is a winner, Alphonse; I feel it in my bones."

Alphonse was not buying it this time. He placed a few francs on the table patted his friend on the back and waved goodbye to the cute little *serveuse* or waitress.

It was unusually warm even though it was mid-day. Alphonse decided a little detour was in order. This time of year, days like this were getting scarce and he planned on taking full advantage. He jumped the little hedge as if he were still a schoolboy and walked the fields in a long circular walk back home. The cows were standing still, an occasional tail whisking off something here and there. The smell of the earth, the fields, the hay, the cows were all intoxicating to him. It had been his life, his passion. It was him. He was the earth. A tightness in his chest made him realize that jumping the fence or that drink had not been such a good idea. He would remember that next time. He came across a row of poplars gently swaying in the breeze. Perhaps just a short stop to catch his breath he thought to himself and then home for lunch before he really got into trouble. Alphonse sat down with his back leaning against the poplar. It was a pretty view, calming yet his heart kept racing. He felt a tightness in his chest. It would go away he thought. He started to sweat. He was worried. His wife would be worried now. He wanted to get up. He could hear things, things that made no sense. Was that his father calling him? Were his brothers nearby? The sky was blue the likes of which he had never seen before. He was incredibly tired now and just wanted to sleep.

THAT SUMMER VACATION LONG AGO

$\mathcal{W}$e spent our first summer in Brittany in Lancieux, a lovely little beach town. It would be another two years before my father found the old place further up the coast. I have written so frequently about it as it were still yet to be discovered by my father on one of his exploratory road trips. Until then, we stayed at a lovely old summer rental in Lancieux, a block from the beach. I was a young boy at the time but to this day have always held fond memories of that summer so long ago. Why that summer, why that place, what was so significant about that period of time? I try not to focus too much on those questions other than to say that I was happy, and I had many pleasant memories. Freud, of course, might have suggested otherwise. The house is still standing I know because I check on it, as I always do, for some reason or another when I am in Brittany having come from the U.S. It's as if I fully expected to encounter my past, to run across that little boy, bucket, and shovel, making his way, determinedly, to the beach or more likely just trailing behind his older brothers.

The town of Lancieux is located approximately 6 miles west of Dinard and it's known as *une station balnéaire* – a beach resort and indeed it is just that. It had then just about everything a family might need to enjoy their *Grandes Vacances*. Up the hill, a newspaper store that also sold post cards outside in a little turnstile, colorful beach chairs and inside, oh that familiar smell that's hard to put one's finger on, maybe it was a combination of newspaper ink, tobacco, dampness, and salty ocean air all rolled into one. On the counter by the cashier was a small stand proudly displaying Mr. *Pierrot Gourmand* himself, a fine fellow indeed but looking slightly worn yet still with his multiple flavored lollypops sticking out, including my favorite, caramel. Next to Pierrot was a box of caramel *Carambars* all neatly lined up and waiting to be picked by someone's sweaty, sticky little hands. There were two little restaurants, though I admit never having seen the inside; an ice cream stand, a bakery, church (the *Eglise de Lancieux*) the *Mairie* and a market every Tuesday – *en saison*, of course. If you wanted more excitement, you were free to drive a little further to the Casino in Dinard or hop the little vedette vert to *St. Malo*. Lancieux's city center was a complex maze of four streets – well at least it had seemed complex at the time but now with over a thousand residents it has become a bustling center of activity.

On a return trip, some years ago, I parked in front of the house and almost at once took the obligatory photos. The house stood firm as a rock, the trim needed painting and the shutters were closed, shut tight, its last renters long since gone. It was after all September and if you were seasonal, you had long packed the last of the beach towels, buckets, and shovels mindful of the *rentrée scolaire* -which heralds the first day of school in France, which also happens during the first week in September. The *rentrée* is a solemn, sacred marker for the state and families throughout France and a date one is not apt to ignore. I venture to say it is most likely codified, enshrined in the Code Napoleon. Yes, it is that important.

Next door to us lived a French family, the husband was a doctor, his wife was American, and they had one boy, André or "*Dédé*" as he was nicknamed. We were both the same age, became fast friends and spent our vacation time on the beach from morning until almost dark, stopping our adventures just long enough to run home for lunch or in afternoon, to enjoy our *gouter*, a snack, on the beach. Wrinkled like two prunes we would sit on the beach and devour those *baguette* sandwiches stuffed with pieces of chocolate or with butter and jam or honey; if we were really lucky, with divine intervention, we had the real thing- *a pain au chocolat* from the bakery. On one occasion, we attacked the rocks covered with mussels and quickly filled several buckets which we brought home as if we were big game hunters. I do not recall ever seeing them after that.

As much fun as we may have had playing on the beach nothing could quite compare with the arrival of the circus! *Le Cirque*

Pander. Weeks before, you would see signs nailed everywhere announcing the grand arrival of the circus. And a grand arrival it was in every sense of the word. The circus troupe would slowly march through town with everything from jugglers, elephants, tigers, stunt men, high-wire family teams, truly an entire cavalcade of glorious talent. But by far the best was when the circus would set up in the big open field directly opposite our house. Everything was within our reach: the ocean, the beach, the field, and the circus. We waited as patiently as we could for the parade to finally make its way down our street towards us as we knew it would. Eventually came the giant elephant leading the parade with its' trainer, a man in white pants, bright red jacket, and black top hat, riding high and twirling a silver baton. We caught as much candy as we could from the clowns, stuffing our pockets in the process, but the fun was just beginning. We watched the circus slowly begin to set up and finally when the big top was up, we all clapped with joy and anticipation. Curiosity got the better of us, hardly a surprise, and of course we just had to poke our heads under the heavy canvas and watch secretly and unobserved the grand process that was unfolding before our very eyes. It was a three-ring circus, in every sense of the word. Animal cages were being set up, nets installed, stunt men testing the high wire; there were a hundred different things going on at once and you wanted to watch each and every one of them intently and not miss anything. We tried to, that is, until our skinny little legs were suddenly dragged out and we found ourselves face to face with someone who could only be the very thing we feared the most in our young lives...A gypsy! I think we made it home in a record time ran upstairs and locked the door and waited.

The arrival of the circus also meant the arrival of *les gitans* or the "gypsies" and right or wrong every parent it seemed was in a heightened state of alert. I am not entirely sure if we really understood what it was all about, but our parents found the idea to be also a convenient way to harness our intense circus curiosity by telling stories of children who had "disappeared" when the circus was in town. Yes, children that is right, they would say almost in a whisper, in one case the Police apparently tracked down the whereabouts of a little boy, Jean Pierre, but he no longer recognized his parents and spoke in a strange dialect. His poor mother was in tears, yes, *c'est terrible*. We always laughed at the stories but for a couple of impressionable kids, the picture had been painted. To this day, I imagine that the man who pulled us out was likely trying save a couple of stupid kids from being crushed by a passing elephant. Oh well, never mind that little detail.

But looking across what was once a field now was a carefully groomed garden with benches. I saw was an elderly man walking his little dog on that sunny late September afternoon. There were still some hardy souls on the beach some sitting on blankets, others playing catch by the water's edge. A windsurfer, wetsuit, and all, was preparing his board. But no children with buckets and shovels digging their way to China, no little boys excitedly pulling off *Moules* from the rocks filling up their buckets for a surprise dinner, no one playing *Tour de France* with marbles on an elaborately built course nor anyone building a sandcastle to stop the tide from coming in once and forever.

It was time to leave. I walked towards town to pick up a postcard. I was out of luck, the tourist store was closed, see you next summer. To help explain the obvious, for example "why is the store closed, I mean it's September?" the French often reply with a shrug of their shoulders followed by "*c'est après la Saison*" (it's after the summer season). It is a useful phrase that explains lots of things not necessarily needing an explanation. I shrugged my shoulders, obviously I should have known better. I found my little Peugeot and followed the *panneau* for *Toutes Directions,* the direction markers, then onto the D786.

Next time, I'll return earlier in the season that way I can catch the trotting races on the beach in late August. Of course, I could also be building that sandcastle.

Lancieux

On Vacation: Roasted Chicken with Lemon and Rosemary or *En Vacance: Poulet Rôti au Citron et au Romarin*

*O*uis mes amis, *les vacances...* and every self-respecting Frenchman with his wife and family are away on vacation. How could you return to Paris not *"bien bronzer"* or appropriately tan?

Gather up your *sandalettes* (awful plastic shoes) and fishing rods. Before you know it, the merry month of August will be upon us heralding the beginning of "*Les Grande Vacances*" that wonderful, much anticipated ritual that's second to none with the possible exception of the "swallows of Capistrano." Paris becomes strangely quiet in some quarters of the city. I know one French couple (they refuse to let me use their names of course!) who actually stay in Paris and enjoy visiting the great monument *historique*, the museums and the parks. They play hard at being a tourist in their own town discovering little places to eat here or to hang out there when normally they never would have the time nor be caught dead doing so. I rather like that idea and often will discover things I never knew about my own town, for example, I didn't know the White House was so close and so white! So, as you madly pack up your *Citroen Deux Chevaux,* or other such luxury vehicle, be sure and remember as you charge onto the *autoroute*, be extra careful as I happen to know from a *flic* friend of mine whose cousin is a *motard* and who regularly works, diligently, the autoroute de Normandy; they especially love this time of year! I won't even begin to talk about the ridiculous fines that are slapped on the average, decent, hard-working Frenchman caught going one *kilometre* above the posted *vitesse*.

Back to food. I have included a little recipe with the collection that you can easily make from the comfort of your rental kitchen, or perhaps in your kitchen trailer or wherever you might find yourselves. It will be well received by everyone after a long full day being at the beach, wandering about in the hills or in town playing tourist, riding your bikes down country roads, or leisurely enjoying a Pastis in the town square. I know which one I would choose.

Coastal West France: An Atlantic Culinary Trilogy

Part 1: The Adventure Begins

This is a wonderful six-part "foodie" trip which starts with first visiting the Opal Coast and the well-known resort of *Le Touquet*. It will be a nostalgic trip for me as the resort is tinged with family stories. Then we will move on to *la Côte Fleurie* or Floral Coast and Deauville and finally ending up in the *Cotes d' Emeraude* in Brittany – be still my heart because I am now in my country now. We will dine in Dinard, one of my favorite towns and not far from the "old place" on the way to the lighthouse at the *Cap Fréhel*. That will conclude the first half of our "foodie" trip.

1.   Le Touquet

I am heading North towards the Opal Coast or more formally known as the *Region-Nord-Pas-de-Calais*. The "Opal Coast" sits between Calais, the first stop of travelers to France from England, and Berk-sur-Mer. Charging along the A16/E402 as fast as I dare, I know full well that at any moment I might have the pleasure of meeting a not too terribly friendly *motard-de-la-gendarmerie* the highway patrol or better yet, the familiar flashing blue lights from a speeding little Renault and a not too amused agent de *la police judiciaire.* I don't think I have enough cash or even a credit card to pay that bill. I could tell him that global warming made me do it, but that might not have the strength to get me off with a white gloved tip to his kepis. My destination is *Le Touquet-Paris-Plage* a wonderful, rather chic, seaside resort dating back to 1912. I suppose one could say that the resort goes back even further to 1874 when *Hippolyte de Villemessant*, the founder of the newspaper "Le Figaro" was given the hard sell to develop the land and call the resort Paris-*Plage*. He bought the idea, and the rest is history.

You might be tempted to ask why I have decided on Le Touquet to start our culinary adventures. Well, truth be known, I remember my father telling me about *Le Touquet*. It was my impression from having listened to him that in those days the town was quite an elegant *station balnéaire* for the well-to-do Parisians who wanted a place to see and, more importantly, to be seen. One gets dreadfully tired of Maxims and the *Tour d'Argent* especially now with all the riff-raft, hardly *comme-il-faut*! We can all agree on that. I do remember seeing a copy a photograph, taken from the European Edition of the New York Herald, which showed my grandmother, my father and his two sisters all posing *en-famille* on the front porch of their summer villa at *Le Touquet* with the caption identifying my grandmother and family and spending the summer of 1929 at their little villa. My little villa looks oddly like a condominium in the U.S. but what do I know. I imagine that my grandfather was likely still in in Paris at their spacious little home on the *Boulevard Suchet* (16th) or likely still on Wall Street. Years later my father noted the villa's name was *Villa Réanne* located on the *avenue de l'Atlantique*. I wanted to see, touch, and feel, taste and write all about it. Call it deep immersion if you will.

If you like art-deco villas, long and wide sandy beaches, good food and while you're at it, throw in a casino for good measure, then *Le Touquet* is a not-to-be missed stop along the Opal Coast. The English know it all to well as it's barely a hop, skip, and jump through the Chunnel, a quick ride down the coast and *voila* you're here. You could probably throw a scone from the White Cliffs and hit the coast or a croissant thrown the other way. *Le Touquet* lies just west of *Étaples-sur-Mer* and south of *Neufchâtel-Hardelot.* I stayed in a quaint little hotel just off the *rue Jean Monnet.* Wonderful, fresh, and clean with an ocean view and, of course, close to restaurants. I need that.

I sniffed around deciding where I would eventually eat and decided on a wonderful little art-deco restaurant, *La Marée Haute* (High Tide) on the *rue Saint Jean.* And was it ever an excellent choice! I started off, quite appropriately, with a chilled bottle of *Muscadet* from the *Val de Loire.* Could I have done otherwise? I suspect not. I then accepted the challenge to start off my meal with the marinated salmon (to die for, thank you very much) and then found myself facing the final two – torn as I was between the *Magret de canard poêlé, pommes poires au jus de cidre* (pan seared duck with apple pears steeped in cider) or the beautiful seared plump scallops simmered in a tarragon butter and white wine reduction sauce. *Monsieur le patron* (who I found out later was originally from St. Brieuc in Brittany – near our old *maison de famille*) assured me the scallops were very fresh – *ce matin-* and indeed most delicious. If a Breton gives you the green light on this dish, then the nod must surely go to the scallops. I thoroughly enjoyed them together with paned-fried Paris potatoes, a tossed green salad, and a selection of cheeses. A nice healthy slice of *Pont L'Évêque* and *Camenbert.*with more sliced baguette, completed this little course to perfection. For dessert, I forced myself and had the incredibly light *crème* brûlée. Heavenly is all I can say. This job is never easy!

To celebrate that wonderful meal, I have included this recipe which comes about as close to the "real thing" short of getting on an Air France flight and joining me, of course.

2.   Deauville, Normandy

As you can imagine, I simply hated leaving Le Touquet with some personal unfinished business, but I must continue on to the second of my three seaside resort visits. I paid my bill and thanked Mme. Veronique, the charming little desk clerk who, I believe, truly hated to see me leave. *Voila*, it is like that sometimes. Stopping at *Jean-Pierre's*, the corner *bar/tabac*, I grabbed a croissant with a super-sized café *au lait* (i.e., two thimbles full) and carefully studied my map. At this time of day, sitting at the café in the morning it was quiet and lovely. I assure you this was not the case in the evening when *le* jukebox was on at maximum volume; it's as if Aznavour or Jacque Brel were in your "*living*" and everything seemed cloudy and blue with cigarette smoke and one too many berets. Anyway, I am heading down the coast towards Normandy because something there is calling me, much like the "swallows of Capistrano" but not quite. Point of reference, my journey will take me on a southerly route away from the Opal Coast to *la Côte Fleurie* or the Flowered Coast, which stretches between the estuaries of the Seine and the Orne Rivers. Road warriors will appreciate the fact that my trusty little Peugeot has been holding out quite well and is simply great in managing the road especially the back roads with those charming blind hairpin turns, and you just hope for the best. For the life of me, I cannot understand how the car rental agency could tell me with a straight face that my car would comfortably hold three passengers, driver, and luggage. "*Non, mais ca ne vas ou quoi?*" Unless, of course, you have four little European dwarfs then by all means throw in the dog and the cat. But more than one American ? *Alors* ça *monsieur, non, pas du tout !*

On this leg of the journey, I swore I would not use my GPS which comes with its own built-in attitude. which upsets me and I tend to, as they say, *appuyer sur le champignon,* as it were. For some reason I find "the voice" a little too smart-assed and condescending for my taste and furthermore I can't stand the reproachful tone when I miss a turn or two, even when I've been warned several thousand meters ahead of time. Therefore, to be a little more creative I am using my 1939 *Guide Michelin Guide du Pneŭ.* I can't imagine things will have changed that much. It is Normandy, lest we forget. A historical note, the Allied forces handed out copies of the 1939 *Guide Mich* to all officers prior to the Normandy landings. Apparently, the Allied High Command was not planning on lovely lunches for the high command but rather feared their progress into French towns and cities would be hampered by the Germans having destroyed all road signs in a fit of efficiency and the *Guide Michelin* just happened to have extremely detailed maps of towns—better than any other maps that were available to the Allies at that time. All-in-all, I must say I did rather well as I navigated with *le Guide.* Granted, I hit a couple of dead ends, drove into a farmhouse courtyard that bore no resemblance to any Marriott Courtyard I ever knew and once even came face-to-face with an unusually large Normand cow who immediately pegged me as an intruder and in a show of fine French diplomacy, promptly turned and showed me its *derrière.* I swore I could hear him laughing. I yelled in English "I've had ruder things happen to me and I will have you for dinner!" Then again in French just in case *la vache normande* didn't get the message. I felt my honor had been saved.

My destination is Deauville, likely the most luxury-minded town of the Flowered Coast and I'm staying at a lovely little mom and pop hotel, the *Hotel Normandy Barrière*, at least that's what I told inquiring minds because I doubted, they would understand my particular need for a seawater spa after a long drive. What is a 5-star hotel for anyway if not to indulge the little folk, such as myself, on those rare occasions? A quick word about the hotel, it's your average run of the mill hotel built in 1912 in that light and airy Anglo-Normand style. You might expect to run into a William the Conqueror or Winston Churchill, arm-in-arm, I mean you just never know. I could see the two of them in sturdy wing chairs comparing invasion tactics. The hotel has hosted all sorts of visitors with familiar names like Sarkozy, Merkel, and Medvedev (sounds to me like a law firm from Hell!) And of course, the usual litany of big screen stars and the average rich and famous who are there because they can. I suppose yours truly wanted to just rub elbows with that patrician *milieu*, eat remarkably well and escape with a relatively intact liver to write my next story, perhaps one from the Emerald Coast.

When I travel, I am somewhat of a creature of habit; rather than constantly buzzing around the glitterati, I like to leave the *beau-monde* and seek out those little off the beaten path restaurants where hopefully I can a place where no one speaks English or awful Russian English. I am funny that way, ask my ex when you have all the time in the world. So, after a little detective work, I found what I was looking for, a charming little establishment with a spectacular menu to beat the band. As I usually do,

I chatted in French with the delightful owners about the weather, the food, the tourists, and the economy of course, could things get any worse, the price of this and that... etc., too many tourists, of course! But since I was *un Américain et non pas un Anglais* they were at first confused how someone could even speak French *comme un Français* that is until I told them my story, Paris, schooling, family, Brittany etc. etc. Expressing relief, they were more than eager to tell me about their prodigal son Philippe who was in California with his technology business (*un* start-up *voyez-vous*).

I began my evening's culinary journey with a half-dozen oysters *Gelée Légère à la Citronnelle* paired very nicely with a chilled white, Burgundy *Côte de Nuits*. A little more chit-chat with Monsieur then I moved on to some simply outstanding *Foie Gras de Canard Vanillé en Robe de Pistaches* -or duck liver *pâté* in a pistachio crust. You could have stuck a fork in me, right then and there, I was that done, *merci*! I should have stopped but I knew in my heart of hearts, I would hate myself in the morning. So, with steely doggedness and my dinner companion, an incredibly attractive bottle of Bordeaux *Médoc,* a young *Pauillac* that I simply could not resist, I ordered the suggested plate – an old standard in Normandy to be sure – but a dish you can never, ever, go wrong, the *Poulet à la Normande.* My choice did not prove me wrong I can assure you. It was a hearty and flavorful dish with the apples, *Calvados,* and fresh cream all dancing wonderfully together with that poor chicken. I emptied the basket of sliced baguette twice so as not waste one single drop of sauce. This main course is very much *du pays* which is how I like to operate on these dangerous missions behind enemy lines, because to do less would mark me as an *étranger* -and please shoot me dead before that ever happens!

On a general note, about my cooking leanings, I usually tend to shy away from *la nouvelle cuisine* as I am not a particularly big fan of two stalks of carrots balanced against a whisper of meager-but tender veal medallion. That is not dinner but maybe an *hors d'oeuvre*! I digress. For dessert, I was content with just a humble slice of apple tart made with those lovely green Normandy apples from the owners' very own orchard. You see them all over Normandy. It was suggested, and I politely agreed, to add just a wee touch of *Calvados* over the apples. After a couple of *expresso* with just whiff of *Calva,* I was ready to do battle in the casino.

There are as many variations on the *Poulet à la Normande* as there are people in Normandy, but I believe this recipe hits the nail of on the head. I hope you enjoy!

3.   Dinard, Brittany

Part one of my most interesting coastal culinary journey finally comes to an end with a stop at a well-known seaside resort in Brittany. It has been a fulfilling journey to say the least! Readers will recall that first we stopped along the Opal Coast at *Le Touquet-Paris-Plage* and had a memorable dinner of scallops in tarragon butter sauce. We then moved south to the Flowered Coast and *Deauville-sur-Mer* where I stayed in an unpretentious little hotel and that evening had a delicious dinner of chicken made Normandy-style paired, paired with a wonderful red wine and a truly memorable dessert and Calvados! Now, last but not least we end this part of our journey with a stop along the Emerald Coast and to one of my favorite, lovely seaside towns, *Dinard*. A glorious, glutinous, and quite fitting temporary end to my culinary travels.

Getting off the N176/E401 I made my way over to the *Route Départementale* D168 (by now my car knew exactly where it was going) and from there across the *Barrage de la Rance* and heading in the general direction of Dinard, *Centre Ville*. If you decide to follow my trail, remember that when you cross the *Barrage* one or both of you has to be sure and steal a glance just long enough to get the full view of the emerald ocean, the brilliant blue sky and St. Malo – *la Cité Corsaire* (pirate city). The view is stupendous and, as the French like to say, "*ça vaut le coup d'oeil.*" It's just too bad one can't stop traffic long enough to take a quick photo. Good luck taking a photo from your car, especially if you are the only passenger. I may have one such photo, just saying.

Dinard is a popular holiday destination on the *Côte d'Émeraude* in Brittany. A former fishing village, it sprawls around the western approaches to the *Rance* estuary, just across from *St-Malo*. While it might not feel out of place on the Côte d'Azur, with its casino, spacious villas and social calendar of regattas and ballet, here in Brittany it's a little incongruous. The nineteenth century shaped the town as it is today due to the influence of the affluent English and Americans.

In the late 19th century American and British aristocrats made Dinard popular as a fashionable summer resort, and they built absolutely stunning villas on the cliff tops and exclusive hotels such as the 'Le Grand Hotel' on the seafront during the French *"Belle Epoque"*. In the late 19th century, the resort became popular with the British wealthy who built magnificent villas on the coast. Dinard rapidly expanded and became the most popular seaside resort in Europe especially for a growing *colonie anglaise* or English expats. It started declining in the 1930s when the Jet set realized the Côte d'Azur also had beautiful weather and all the time. Today, Dinard is considered one of the most "British" of seaside resorts in France; however, it has still managed to retain its French charm. I once remarked to a British expat who was quite familiar with Dinard that there certainly seemed to be more British expats in Dinard these days; she replied, without breaking her stride, "you know we say the same thing about the French." Wonderful story and says it all quite nicely.

I found a perfectly marvelous place to stay overnight. The Hôtel De La Vallée on 6 Avenue George V. It is moderately priced, friendly and efficient staff. Easy access to restaurants. For a night it was more than I needed. But, after all, a little indulgence never hurt anyone.

The waterfront structures are, with the exception of the Casino Barriere Dinard at 4 boulevard Wilson, beautiful Victorian villas rather than just your plain hotels or shops, overlook the large sandy beaches that attracts the summer crowd each year. I have been going to Dinard, off and on, ever since 1959 when my parents purchased their little *propriété* aka *Maison de Maitre*- some forty minutes from Dinard. I loved going then and love going to this day.

There has been some talk about a family member who lived in Dinard in the 1930's and 1940's and who, as I understand got caught up by the Germans and interned. I am still searching to nail that little detail down. It will be a fun challenge.

I had some time on my hands before wrestling with the serious matter of diner selections and since the weather was agreeable, I made a little *pèlerinage* or pilgrimage up a hilly side-street, past homes cloistered away from prying eyes, until I finally reached my destination, the *rue Faber* and from there made a right turn onto avenue George Clemenceau and into St Bartholomew's Anglican Church. St. Barts, as it's known, is truly a beautiful little church and once inside the perimeter wall, by the little gate, is a small brass plaque in honor of my mother who greatly enjoyed attending Sunday services there. There is a wall inside with all the names of those soldiers who lost their lives in WWI and II. I suppose for me, it is just something I do when I am in Dinard, and certainly after a lengthy absence.

It was time to think all about dinner in Dinard. I stopped at the Balneum, a *salon de thé* right off the Avenue George Clemenceau and sat outside with a pot of tea and English biscuits, (it all seemed so appropriate, somehow) and enjoyed the wonderful ocean view. I sifted through my research and one thing was clear, seafood in one form or another was once again going to be part of my diner. Brittany is a region of windswept, rugged shorelines, known for its fisherman since ancient times and nowhere in France, in my humble opinion, can you find a more tempting array of seafood the likes of John Dory, Hake, Cod, and Mackerel along with shellfish such as clams, mussels, scallops, spider crabs, lobster and crayfish. I perused my 1939 *Guide Michelin* for any helpful hints and was particularly taken by one menu which advertised *Langouste Emeraude* which sounded delicious, or it was the 1931 *Chateau Mouton Rothschild*. Sadly, the restaurant, the dinner special and wine had long since gone.

Diner at last!!

I finally found my little restaurant, *La Marmite du Pêcheur*, the fisherman's stew pot, tucked away from the hustle and bustle of Dinard's immediate downtown yet with enough of a view of beautiful *St. Malo* and the bay to keep me happy. My research (a more updated

Guide) told me it was considered *"une bonne adresse a Dinard"* and indeed it proved to be that and a whole lot more. *La Marmite* was about as close to an authentic *petit bouchon* as one might find when dining in Lyon. All the fineries of Brittany were on display from the linen tablecloths, salt and pepper shakers and sugar bowls all Quimper (full disclosure: Maybe I have or two or more Quimper pieces including a bowl with my very own name inscribed on it, of course!) There were heavy water glasses from another era that could have been used as a weapon. On the wall, the centerpiece was a large blackboard with *les plats du jour* and the various catches of the day. Everything spelled "super fresh" – from the sea to me. On either side of the blackboard were old photographs of fishermen displaying their catch and looking serious but quite pleased; there were photos of *vieux Dinard* and *St. Malo* hearkening back to time long ago. In the background, music softly playing an unmistakably local Breton seafaring tune. Yes, I had arrived.

St Malo as viewed from Dinard

I started with a bottle of chilled 2008 *Muscadet de Breizh* which is the only wine native to all of Brittany and it even has its own *appellation d'origine contrôlée* (A.O.C.) ever since 1936. I told the young lady to order a glass for monsieur who was behind the little zinc-covered bar and clearly the owner-in-charge. I find a little gesture helps smooth out one's meal. I surveyed the chalk board to see what the immediate future held for my appetite. The evening special besides a host of other delights was *La Cotriade d'Armor* or a fish stew from the Armorican coast. Remy, the owner gave me the local thumbs up on this dish and told me that a *Cotriade* is to Brittany what a bouillabaisse is to Marseilles and furthermore that *Cotriade* recipes are as varied as the Breton coastline itself. The dish was originally prepared at sea so you can imagine it was a rather rustic meal made with whatever was caught that day, potatoes, a lot of spices, and sea water all boiled together. This truly local dish is slowly making a comeback and for that I'm certainly thankful.

I teased my appetite by starting with "*Le Plateau Dégustation*" a varietal platter of fresh oysters from the bay. I toyed for a moment with the crayfish and mayonnaise as an appetizer but decided to hold for the main course. Finally, the *plats de résistance*, the main event, the Cotriade arrived with Madame right behind looking immensely pleased with herself; I made sure there were plenty of "ooohs" and "aaahs" on my end. Indeed, the *Cotriade* is a meal to be reckoned with and not one for the idle tourist, *ahh, non monsieur.* The dish had an exotic smoky aroma, a combination of seafood, spices, garlic, and smoked bacon. It was that and so much more. I struggled my way through the oversize bowl that was filled to the very edge and with the help of baskets of crusty bread, I am proud to say that I continue to be a member in good standing of the clean plate club.

Having survived that part of the meal and being a better person for it, I was presented with the dessert menu. All the selections seemed to blur except for one item: *Île flottante géant* or floating island – a desert that took me racing back to my childhood in Paris when my mother would bring it to the table with great flourish and too much clapping, all around. It was time to answer the clarion call, to rise and accept the challenge. I did and beautifully so I might add. Floating island is a French dessert consisting of meringues floating on *crème anglaise* (a vanilla custard). The meringues are prepared from whipped egg whites, sugar and vanilla extract then quickly poached. The *crème anglaise* is prepared with the egg yolks, vanilla, and hot milk, briefly cooked.

Later, after the paramedics had gone, I relaxed over black coffee and a snifter of Courvoisier and recalled my wonderful whirlwind tour of these three coastal jewels now at an end and pondered how soon before my return to the Emerald Coast.

SCALLOPS GRATINÉES OR GRATINÉE DE COQUILLE ST JACQUES

I will admit that I had every good intention of stopping after the delightful meal I had in Dinard with a beautiful dinner view of St. Malot, *ville corsair*, or pirate city. I find it necessary to talk about a meal that I would recommend to anyone if they were to find themselves in St. Malot. This is simply marvelous dish!

Coquille St Jacques or *pecten maximus* (to you and I) are scallops baked in a butter cream and Parmesan sauce. This dish is celebrated in many locations in France, particularly in Normandy and of course, Brittany. It's the latter that has me in this state of barely controlled, culinary excitement. The Coquille Saint-Jacques fisherman here take to the waters between November and April and fish on the bottom of the *baie de Saint-Brieuc*. Every year, 1500 tons of scallops or more are unloaded on the docs, weighed, and auctioned off.

The restaurant where I have had some fine coquilles as a child and later as an adult is *A La Duchesse Anne* in the very heart of St. Malot, *Cité Corsaire*. Here the dish is made with a delightful added little touch of muscadet wine. Perhaps what is even more delightful is a late lunch at the *Duchesse Anne* on a still warm, late September afternoon then work off that wonderful meal with a little tour in town or a walk on the ramparts, where they say pirates still lurk. By end of September a lot of the annoying tourists are gone but some can still be found lurking here and there.

A quick note. Clever foodies may have noted that Coquilles Saint Jacques could be less ceremoniously called "Scallops in a Sauce Parisienne." Sauce Parisienne is the same as *Sauce Allemande,* but you won't find me calling it by either one of those names. It is what it is. I like to think of Coquilles Saint-Jacques as scallops on display in a heavenly rich mixture of butter, cream, mushrooms, and Parmesan cheese, and baked in a scallop shell. A little white wine for added flavor is a must. I am in Heaven!

Part 2: The Adventure Continues

An Introduction

This is a follow-on to our most excellent culinary adventure in Northern and Western France which took us, as you may recall, to Le Touquet on the Opal Coast, then down to Deauville on the Flower Coast in Normandy and lastly, ending in Dinard on Brittany's beautiful Emerald Coast. Now, dear readers, just when you thought your liver and arteries were no longer going to be in harms-way, indulge me, if you will as we stretch beyond the Brittany coast. We continue our journey, always staying true to finding interesting resorts, fascinating places that are often steeped in history and of course all with plenty of outstanding regional food and wine. All of this can be found along France's southwestern Atlantic coast.

First, we will be in Cap Ferret, a less well-known seaside resort on an incredibly fabulous and windswept, pine-covered peninsula along France's *Côte d'Argent* (the Silver Coast.) It is a simply fascinating locale, quite unique with incredible culinary diversity and I think, an ambiance that will knock your socks off. You heard it here first! A special place indeed. Second, we will be going to one of my favorite towns, Grand Biarritz on the Cote des Basques. It is steeped in history and well worth visiting and a short hop over the border will find you in San Sebastian, Spain, another gem of a resort! Our last stop along France's west Atlantic coast will be Saint-Jean-de-Luz. While still a part of the Cote des Basques and close to Biarritz, Saint-Jean-de Luz is quite unique, and the quintessential picturesque seaport town nestled in Basque country. I have a soft spot for anything that is Basque. Not too hard to figure me out.

4. Cap Ferret in Gironde on the Atlantic Coast

Cape Ferret is ideally situated on the beautiful *Côte d'Argent*, on a long lick of land along the Atlantic coast and just under an hour's drive due west of Bordeaux. The *Côte d'Argent*, in case you are simply dying of curiosity, just happens to be the longest and sandiest stretch of coastline in Europe, running from the mouth of the Gironde at Royan below La Rochelle all the way down to fashionable Biarritz. Now there's a free cocktail factoid for you.

At the onset, let me state for the record that I did not know that much, if anything, about Cap Ferret oftentimes guilty of confusing it with Cap Ferrat as in Saint Jean-Cap Ferrat, that luxury resort on the Riviera, the Cote d'Azur, the summer playground of the idle rich and famous and where I am usually seen. Cap Ferret, on the other hand, stands in stark contrast, it has none of that shimmering, over the top, glitz, and glamor, at least not yet and hopefully maybe never. Real estate prices, I understand, are climbing which is a sure indication monied interests are moving in. Sad. If you are searching for a unique seaside getaway that is "out of the way" for sure, then Cap Ferret is the perfect place; it has a long sandy bay, protected from the Atlantic waves by huge sea walls, it has beaches just a little further away for those who brought their surfboards seeking the challenge of the rolling and pounding Atlantic surf. There is no claim to fame here, no stories about Charlie Chaplin, Pablo Picasso, or other celebrities, no sir, not here. Cap Ferret's perhaps biggest claim to fame has to be its booming oyster farming industry and an unbeatable, magnificent view across the *Arcachon* Bay, and the towering, monstrous *Dune du Pilat*, Europe's tallest sand dune. Some wags unfortunately have taken it upon themselves to compare it to the Hamptons. All I can say is "I hope the Hell not!" and please excuse my French. Because who wants any of that self-absorbed, sleazy riff-raft around here anyway? It sets an awful example for the children. If pushed, I would say that Cap Ferret is more along the lines of a Cape Cod in terms of charm and where good seafood always reigns supreme.

I arrived late afternoon and made my way to my hotel which turned out to be a clear winner in my book. The *Hotel Maison du Basin* had been advertised as:

"Une ancienne maison de forestier joliment restaurée en un hôtel de charme pour le plaisir de vous offrir une parenthèse de douceur."

Roughly speaking, the house had been, at one time, a caretaker's residence but long and since then, lovingly restored into a charming hotel. How best to describe the unique ambiance? Perhaps a

Kennedy summer retreat (I mean who does not summer there?) with white linen, sisal rugs everywhere, polished wood walls and nautical paintings at every turn. The outside is painted a forest green, and the veranda is framed by blue French doors with tropical flowers everywhere. It was entirely possible that I could have run into Hemingway or Fitzgerald because it had, to me at least, that ambiance one often associates with the Lost Generation. You either get it or you don't. I felt I should have brought my tropical white linen suit and my Panama hat. Everything screamed that part of the world, I loved it and wanted more.

Lucky me I was able to reserve one of the eleven rooms that make up this hotel though mine was, shall we say, at the entry level, which is fine by me although I'm not saying I would have turned up my nose at the deluxe room, no sir, I have some standards. For now, I had a far more important agenda ahead of me, specifically where was I going to have dinner? I had read and researched well-ahead a few of the restaurants on the Cap though none of them were ever mentioned in my 1939 *Guide Michelin*, so I had to do things the old-fashioned way and improvise.

I saw very quickly that I was going to have a real problem choosing where to finally land; I wanted to try every little restaurant along the way, one more delicious sounding than the next. One in particular was *Chez Hortense* because this was clearly a Cap Ferret institution that had been in the same family for four generations. You don't make that marker by selling lousy food and providing exceptionally bad service. The popular fare, it seemed as I observed customers settling down *a table*, was a big bowl of mussels *"façon Hortense."* The mussels arrived mixed with a mixture of serrano ham, sausage, garlic, butter, and white wine. It made my mouth water. The other popular dish seemed to be the grilled turbot which came with *allumette* fries in a mountain high pile. How delightfully unpretentious, very much like where diners were seated at rickety wooden tables on a terrace overlooking *Arcachon* Bay. I held myself in check, it was killing me. I was going to return to the bar/bistro/restaurant at my hotel *Maison du Basin*. Oh, such a smart move that proved to be. Later, I even patted myself on the back.

My first stop was *Le Tchanqué* a bar set-off from the main restaurant. It had that un-mistakable feel to it, you could have been somewhere in the Florida Keys, maybe even old Havana, or Jamaica. With an iced-cold *Bière artisanale Gasconha (Pessac, craft beer)* I prepared my pre-dinner plan of attack. I decided that, as a salute to my locale, it would be important to start off with a half dozen raw and half dozen grilled oysters straight from the *Arcachon* Bay, this would get things rolling. The oysters were magnificent, and I especially liked the grilled oysters with *Pommeau*. These beauties arrived table side, the grilled oysters having just been drizzled over with an equal amount of melted butter then drizzled again but with an equal amount of *Pommeau*, an apple brandy-calvados mixture. Calling for seconds was so easy.

The bar menu had quite a selection of what are known as *Pinchos*, also known as *Pintxos*, a traditional small snack from the Basque country, typically eaten in bars and traditional fare in northern Spain. To be polite, I ordered a sampler plate of these mysterious creatures, how could I not? They arrived, slices of crusty bread with a variety of toppings, salmon on one, fresh tuna another, one with smoked ham and goat cheese, one with blue cheese and walnuts that I found outrageously delicious, and the last one, a slice of garlicky salami with baby *cornichon* and a smoky jam base (yes it was to die for as well, thank you.) Before I knew it, another beer had mysteriously landed at my table.

What new culinary adventure would my dinner bring? I could have done the sensible thing for once in my life and stopped my culinary excess at once. I could have sat on the porch in a comfortable white wicker armchair, immersed in a good book, enjoying the sea breeze, and later perhaps a Cognac or two before bed. I could have chosen a lot of sensible things but much like a moth attracted to light, I knew if had to continue my culinary quest not wanting to face the thought of defeat and humiliation come morning.

Dinner menu at the main hotel restaurant was a challenge. On the one hand I wanted to stay true to the *Cuisine du Pays* if you will, leaning on specialties that were local or at least local to the region. Arguably, I felt I had already made a good dent with local oysters, a few *Pinchos* and aggressively sampling the craft brews. I knew that more was expected of me. The menu was a healthy mix of French classics including *foie gras terrine, coquilles St Jacques* (an old favorite) and duck confit. One thing I did settle on and early, was my dinner companion, though short-lived, she was a nicely chilled *Blanc-Cotes De Gascogne*, I must say the two of us got along famously and right from the start too. That is so important, granted the conversation may have been a little one sided. It was a difficult decision having to choose between the *Terrine de foie gras mi-cuit au vin rouge* or the *Tartare de saumon et avocat, chantilly au citron*. I choose carefully and went for the *foie gras* selection as it's one of my weaknesses. It was light, incredibly tasty and all around superb. You could have taken the plate back and used it again, it was that clean!

By this time, my dinner partner had long since passed out, her head in an ice bucket. I replaced her (how cavalier of me, I know) with an old favorite of mine who just happened to be in the area *Entre-deux-Mers* (*Château Turcaud*). For the main course, the decision again was not an easy one. I was torn between *Coquille St Jacques* roasted in *demi-sel* butter with an apple celery salad with cider vinaigrette dressing and walnuts. Or perhaps the *Cuisse de canard conte,* Tartare marinated duck breast in a Thai broth served with crunchy vegetables drizzled over with olive oil or cream. You choose. The duck breast won the day! By this time, I could have been led away on a stretcher right then and there. But the night was young, and a dessert menu was promptly presented and yes, I just looked. Finally, after someone finally stopped twisting my arm, I choose the *Tarte Tatin,* a wonderful pastry dish in which the fruit is caramelized in butter and sugar (sure why not?) before the tart is baked.

Stick a fork in me, I was done, as the saying goes. I strolled over to *Le Tchanqué* and ordered a *Diplomatico Gran Reserva* a Venezuelan rum, two ice cubes and a slice of lime. This rum is probably among the best I have ever tasted, and I have tasted, shall we say, more than one or two. I sat out on the porch, enjoying the cool evening breeze, from somewhere out in the darkness I could hear the unmistakable voice of Aznavour, the music, his voice drifted over. It was an evening to remember; I marveled over the uniqueness of this incredibly special part of France.

I checked out of the hotel the next morning feeling as if, maybe, I had put on a few French pounds. Madame, who was behind the counter suggested that since I was not planning on having breakfast at the hotel that I absolutely must, on my way out of town, stop at *Chez Pascal, 46 Route Cap Ferret* where her sister worked but warned me that I had better leave right away because it was a popular breakfast stop with the tourists. She was true to her word, when I arrived there was already a line forming at the front door of this roadside bakery. This bakery is famous for its baguettes but more so for its addictive *Dunes Blanches*, bite-size pastries of flaky dough topped with crystallized sugar and filled with an airy cream. You can choose from six flavors, including Nutella, salted caramel, and sesame nougat.

I ordered one in each flavor. It could be a long time before my next stop.

5. Grand Biarritz on the Atlantic coast

French history is leading me directly to the "Pearl of the Basque Coast" at least I hope so as I continue to navigate using my 1939 Guide Michelin. Following a few twists and turns, I am able to find the A63 going south, and I am sticking to it like glue. To get to my destination, I traveled through some interesting territory, *Les Landes de Gascogne.*to be more precise. The Natural Park is a protected area of pine forest, wetland, and oceanic coastline but in all honesty, as nice as that may be, this area is most famous for the hero of *Alexandre Dumas's musketeer* books the man from Gascony called, non-other than, *D'Artagnan.* As a kid I could not get enough of the Three Musketeers, or Cardinal Richelieu and his scheming treacherous plots and whispering into the Kings' ear, of course palace intrigue inevitably ended with a swashbuckling sword fight and the Musketeers heroically holding off a dozen of the Cardinal's men. Yes, justice!! Getting back on track, the 'fourth' musketeer actually lived in Gascony as did Athos, Porthos and Aramis. So, buckle up with that tasty tidbit of cocktail party factoid, we are going to step into history, and you can bet your plumed musketeer's hat! You cannot forget such names as Eleanor of Aquitaine, Philip II, Henry III, and the "kindly" Plantagenets Kings who never tired of helping their enemies separate from their heads. It is like taking French history all over again but maybe this time I will do better and not get my exam papers thrown at me by *Madame de la torture,* the torture teacher. I thought a little bit of French history certainly trumped a guided visit to *Les Landes.*

Where exactly am I heading, other than due south? To a favorite destination of mine, Biarritz, a city with an undeniable vibrancy to it, rich in culture, tradition and especially the gourmet food. I was thinking that those Vikings knew a good thing when they landed in the region back in 840. Many most likely tired of the plundering decided to hang up their memories of the frozen fjords and settle down in Biarritz, eat well, marry a local, and play golf. It's a historical guess on my part to be sure but my ever-keen revisionist sense of history leads me to believe that just maybe Biarritz was after the last town on the Viking's "plunder and burn" list or just maybe the casino was open by then. What a draw!

In 1843, a gentlemen by the name of Victor Hugo, no, not the butcher down the street, nor the contract employee on your payroll but the author, once referred to Biarritz as a "charming and beautiful place" but what was perhaps more worrisome for Mr. Victor was his grave fear that Biarritz "would become fashionable." From gambling Vikings to Princess Eugenie, Queen Victoria, Edward VII, and the Grand Casino, it was just a short hop to Biarritz calling itself the "queen of resorts and resorts of kings." Today Grand Biarritz is one of France's most famous seaside resorts and up to the 1950s was indeed the playground of the rich, the aristocracy, royalty, and movie stars. Created by Napoleon III the glitterati soon came to gamble at the Casino, to eat in the numerous restaurants and to see and be seen in the iconic hotels that graced the city. The rise of the *Cote d'Azur* as the new place to be and be seen dampened Biarritz as a resort much like her sister resorts further north along the coast. By the 1990's the city has gradually come back to life with the help of international surfers and competitions, families, and tourists. Today, Biarritz, this beautiful gem, is once again sparkling, smart and fun.

More importantly than this heady royal mixture is the fact we are in Basque country home of some of the most interesting dishes and spices that are to beat the band, as they say. As soon as I know there is Basque cuisine, I am off like a dog heading for home. Do not try to stop me.

Having done a little bit of research, I was slightly ahead of the game in finding a cozy little hotel, unpretentious and welcoming. And I found it at the *Hotel Saint-Julien* on the Avenue Carnot. This place is on a quiet street (bonus points) and not at all far from the city center (bonus point) I do not need to drive or get a cab. I pleaded with madame behind the desk for a room on one of the upper floors because I wanted a view of the sea. For a few Euro's more, it's worth it, I was in luck. The *Saint-Julien* only serves breakfast which was fine by me given my timetable. I will tell you it was my kind of breakfast, beautifully presented with fresh fruit, an abundance of fresh croissants and choice of eggs any darn way you want it. Having settled in my room, I opened the windows taking in the full the view and breathing the wonderful air. I decided it was time to go hunting for a great dinner spot.

Dinner Calls

Within a few a blocks from my hotel I found an interesting spot, LTB La Table Basque, on the Avenue de la Marne. As I have noted quite often, Basque cooking is a trigger for me, it is something I cannot resist. I am only human after all. This particular regional cooking represents for me a collection of savory spicy flavors and rich aromas and more; it's about lamb and beef that's grilled over hot coals, delicious lamb stews, red spicy, smoky pimento de *Espelette* (unique to Basque region) *Idiazabal* sheep's cheese, and of course *txakoli* (sparkling white-wine).

Oh, that most delicious moment when you peruse a menu, which I love, but never-ever with a parched throat. I ordered a bottle of Jurancon sec, knowing a little bit, as I do, about this particular appellation tucked away in the foothills of the

Pyrenees or more precisely in the commune of Jurancon. My dinner companion arrived just in time, in all her splendor, chilled (such is life) to perfection along with a little plate of black and green olives, pickled garlic, and baby *cornichons*. I could have ordered two more of those plates, but I was trying to keep myself somewhat in check.

What a menu, what a challenge! For starters, I was torn between the *Assiette de Jambon* Serrano or the *Assiette du Terroir*. Being the natural little piggy that I am, I jumped at the *Assiette du Terroir*. Seriously, wouldn't you? it came with thick slice of *Pâté Basque,* seven (that's right) distinct kinds of ham, dried Spanish pork and *saucisson sec.* Added to this was an assortment of little gherkins and peppers. Yes, it was certainly a lot to finish however let me remind you that this is not just an idle sport for gentlemen. We are talking serious business. If you do not come prepared, you best go home.

For the main course it was a challenge indeed between a Basque-style grilled lamb and the grilled salmon with lemon butter and a Basque spicy tomato-pepper sauce. Yes, tough choices indeed. I would love to have had portions of each, but the waiter smiled at me and shook his head as if saying "do I look like I was born yesterday? Not only no but Hell no." I got the drift and boldly ordered a repeat on the wine which seemed to have disappeared and opting for the grilled lamb and side vegetables. Holy Toledo Batman this is a dish for kings! The way they cook this poor little lamb is to brown the outside, slightly crispy yet searing in the juices. Cooking la *plancha* is a rustic preparation that guarantees keeping the interior of the meat moist, tender, and juicy while the outside crispy and flavorful.

For dessert I opted to play it safe and chose *the Nougat glacé au touron, coulis de framboises* a lovely little ice cream concoction with nougat, a mixture of honey, roasted nuts, and candied fruits.

To cap off my evening, an *Izarra* seemed particularly fitting. It's a traditional herbs liqueur native to the Pyrenees, in other words typical of the French Basque Country. They come in different varieties but the most common is the yellow *Izarra* (with an infusion of saffron). A unique, tasty, and quite different experience. What better way to close out my evening.

It was a beautiful cool evening, and I took a long, casual walk back to the Hotel Saint-Julien by way of the oceanfront, passing stately properties that overlooked the wide expanse of the beautiful Biarritz beach.

6. Saint-Jean-de-Luz

My final destination was just a hop skip and jump away from Biarritz. I am thankful, especially after all the miles I have put on this rental jalopy.

You may recall from your history class (I had trouble remembering anything that had to do with studies) thus I was marked early on by French Administration as someone doomed to always be "*le petit dernier*" they probably already saw me with my green maintenance jacket (Ville de Paris stenciled somewhere in case I tried to escape) and a sturdy broom. Back to history, it was in 1660 when Louis XIV chose this tiny fishing village along the coast between Biarritz and the Spanish border, as the place to marry the *Infanta* Maria Teresa of Spain. Get ready, useless cocktail factoid coming your way: Back in the day, Saint-Jean-de-Luz was known for being a city of *corsaires* or pirates and English sailors would refer to the town as the "Viper's Nest." That was for me an immediate draw. Saint-Jean- de Luz is the quintessential picturesque seaport town with lovely houses, hotels, casinos, bars, and restaurants sprinkled along the waterfront. How could you not love this place?

My research led me to choose the *hôtel La Devinière, "un hotel de charme"* and quite aptly put! Once the home of writer François Rabelais, this quaint hotel is on a pedestrian street right in the middle of the historic center. It is a two-minute walk from the nearest beach if I felt so inclined but more importantly it was close to the restaurant scene. Now, I will admit under oath, that one of the reasons for choosing this particular hotel was its name as it rang a nostalgic bell deep in me from somewhere long ago, on another continent, thousands of miles away. The *Devinière* that I recalled had been a lovely restaurant nestled in the slopes of the Binza hills in Kinshasa, formerly known, back in my day, as Leopoldville. In fact, the restaurant was just a short hop from where we lived, quite comfortably, in a neighborhood called *Ma Campagne.* The restaurant afforded a spectacular view of the city and the Congo River rapids. I shall say no more other than the name took me, with the speed of greased lightning, to another time and place. Congo hands (missionaries, embassy, business) knowledgeable of this area would, most likely, nod their heads and smile.

My intelligence source (i.e., Madame, behind the desk) suggested a restaurant, which was a diamond in the rough, she claimed, with excellent seafood prepared by a decent chef. That pretty much sealed it for me, I thanked Madame, dropped my bags in the room, admired the view, made sure everything was working and off I went to find this diamond in the rough.

The restaurant's name is a grabber let alone my trying to pronounce it. Restaurant Pilpil-Enea on 3 rue Sallagoity. A busy little restaurant tucked away down a quiet side street.

I will let you in on the back-story to the name Pilpil; I immediately thought it would reference a cousin of the Pili-Pili variety that hot African sauce that can easily blow you head off. No, the Pilpil is a Basque, big, flavored sauce. Traditionally it's made by cooking skin-on fillets of salt cod (bacalao) in garlic-infused oil. Once the fish is removed, the milky white protein traces left behind are whisked into a sauce to emulsify them with the garlic oil. So, you have salt cod, garlic, chilies and olive oil, and constant motion which allows the olive oil and salt cod to emulsify into the fantastic pil-pil sauce.

Back to the restaurant itself. I am not one that jumps to conclusions, but I will admit on entering the restaurant, I thought I might have miscalculated and would have to fall on sword if that had been the case. Here's why. It looks a bit rough around the edges, (yes, I know something about judging a book and its cover) but to its credits, this old-school restaurant made up for its lack of finesse and nose in the air with tons of nautical atmosphere: fishing nets, oil lanterns, wooden tables and checked tablecloths. The only thing missing was a boat.

It was certainly cozy, but cozy can also be a double-edge sword. The tables were a little close to each other for my taste. Imagine my delight on finding that the lovely couple to my right were from Stratford-upon-Avon. Lovely people, just delightful, even and I told them how much I enjoyed Stratford and in fact, one my ancestors came from the small village of Byford in Herefordshire, several centuries ago, that would be before my time. To my left, as only my luck would have it, was a Russian couple who spoke terrible French and the gentlemen's English was just shy of half an alphabet. For all I knew, he could have been formerly associated with the KGB or the GRU, he had that welcoming Slavic look complete with pale skin and dead grey eyes one sees on sharks. I imagined he never had a moment's hesitation in his life when it came to eliminating his prey. While his companion, a much younger, very attractive lady and who was surely his daughter, was delightful. Note to self: I must remember to revisit France where the French can actually be found.

I decided I would start with the *Soupe de Poissons Garnie Maison* with asparagus and baby *pommes de terre fondants*. Spectacular choice I might add. On the board, the owner had suggested two wines, a red and white *Irouleguy* which is a small wine region located 125 miles south of Bordeaux in the French Basque Country. Here, you are about as far south in France as is possible before actually crossing the Pyrenees Mountains into the Pais Vasco of northern Spain. The white wine was a Xuri blanc, *Irouleguy*. Totally appropriate.

Both my dinning partners were struggling with parts of the menu, so yes, because I am nice American guy, I first helped my British cousins then turned to the young Russian glamour girl who was sporting a mile-long pout for having had to wait for my help. We chatted, she found me amusing, I found her to be kryptonite. Valuing my life and not wishing to end up as some fishermen chum the next morning, I turned my attention to my own menu and said nothing further.

More wine! I can't study a menu without a glass of wine. It's an occupational hazard of sorts so I gave in, weak that I am, and ordered a bottle of Madiran red from the village with the same name, in the gently rolling countryside of Gascony in Southwest France. Perusing the menu, I saw it staring at me, beckoning me with a wink as someone might do in back, darken alleys of Pigalle. La Parillada, a grilled fish sampler "a *la chancha*." It was that or the Merlu (Cod) *à l'Espagnole* which sounded equally delicious. La Parillada consisted of just a few things: shrimp, mussels, cod, prawns, roasted garlic, and deliciously sweet potatoes. Wonderful, crunchy bread to mop everything. Leave nothing behind! It was just amazing and for a seafood lover like myself, I was in seventh heaven.

After easing my belt, it was on to desert. This time I went easy on myself and ordered a Koka which is a *Flan Basque* with an added touch of rum and vanilla flavored bourbon. When one is on a roll, it's best to keep on that way.

I took a nice leisurely stroll back to my hotel and keeping an eye out for the Russian. You can never be too careful

My comfy, overstuffed bed was calling me, how could I resist?

For tomorrow I had accepted an invitation from my good friend Luc, aka "four fingers" and his lovely wife Anais to stay an extra few days in Saint-Jean-de- Luz. She is an outstanding cook, and he is a former "Para" who operated behind the lines in West Africa, so he tells me. I love his stories and you never knew if they were fact or fiction. Both are all around "bon-vivant." I have much to look forward to.

More (Modern Day) Memories Made in Brittany

I have written plenty on a topics that is near and dear to my heart: Brittany and with it, the wonderful regional cuisine. All are part and parcel to so many of my stories in this book. It's not at all surprising after spending so many years in France as a child that I would later have returned as often as possible. My memories of those summers and a few rugged winters thrown in for good measure at our family's 19th century stone country home tucked away in a little village along Brittany's Emerald Coast have been forever seared in my soul. Naturally, the house, the land, the food, the people, and my stories, are all intertwined in this book, as it must be.

When I'm lucky enough to return to the family home, I make a point of visiting all the little nooks and crannies that I so vividly recall from those many summers back in the 1960's and 1970's when we were all together as a family, my brothers, and sisters. For some reason, my mind is forever fixed at some in the past, a time long ago. It's how I remember it; it gives me a degree of comfort and perhaps it's how I come to terms with the inevitable passage of time. I can recall as if it were yesterday, our dear cook, Simone: *"À table tout le monde"* and a delicious meal would surely follow.

To be quite honest, returning to Brittany, one hopes for no real drastic changes either to the house or the little country village. But there has been change. Thanks to my brother, there have been some needed and welcomed improvements to the house. So thankful for that. Other changes have come about naturally and out of necessity. These days we no longer use the well that still sits in the graveled courtyard in front of the house. My parents wisely realized that perhaps three boys playing in the general vicinity of any well was probably not a good idea. To be sure, we regularly lifted the then old rotting cover only to throw down bits of gravel or perhaps a rotting fig or something larger perhaps like someone's tennis shoe as payback, *"go get it if you want it."* We would all wait and listen for the inevitable plop, splash, and then smile. Of course, we often wondered if the old water bucket and chain could have held one scared cat, a dog or maybe the youngest brother. That's when I, as if on cue, would disappear in thin air. The outhouse which once stood, ever so proudly, out by the garden wall is of course no longer there. The original garden stands as it always has. The gnarled apple and pear trees still line the graveled walk to the *potager*. The tree from which more than one duck or rabbit was given its last rites is still there standing and our fort that proudly few the Confederate battle flag, sewed with loving care by my mother, her heart forever in North Carolina, is now long gone. I should note that my brother somehow kept the flag and framed it and it hangs proudly on one of the bedroom walls. Nowhere are the spirit of my parents as strong and enduring as it is they were here on the little piece of earth.

A rapid communications system to announce lunch.

I would note that my mother and Simone always enjoyed a close relationship. At times they acted more as if they were sisters. Years later I recalled that it was Simone who brought to my mother's attention a strange lump on her back. In many ways that was the beginning of the end. Eventually our mother passed away, in her early sixties, from cancer. Much too young. As strange as this may seem, and I can't speak for my siblings, I never really knew my mother or my father or for that matter ever really got close to them. Both were difficult to know and not always that open. Nevertheless, the house in Brittany is full of tender stories as well as, of course, difficult ones.

My mother, in a rare moment, relaxing in the back
garden with a cup of tea. Brittany, circa 1970.

Inside the house, the kitchen and bathroom have thankfully seen more than a few changes. For example, in the kitchen we no longer use a "*Garde Manger*" which is basically a screened-in food storage area which held cheese, butter, milk, perhaps leftovers. Interestingly enough, the term "*garde manger*" originated in pre-Revolutionary France and I don't mean 1968 either. Growing up my parents never purchased food in mass quantities instead, my mother, with her netted grocery bag, would dutifully walk down to the village each and every day and that was the way it was. Just as I had seen her do it each and every day in Paris. The bathroom has thankfully replaced the outhouse. Having a tub was a wonderful thing but it was easily surpassed when I learned that a shower had been installed. Would modern day wonders never cease?

After dropping my bags, I would usually scoot out for a drive along the coast admiring the view and the wide beaches. My first stop was always the lighthouse, and I would stroll out to the point and gulp in the incredibly fresh sea air and take in the vista -a breathtaking coastline. To be sure, I would snap my share of photographs as if for some reason I expected the coastline to change yet nothing really had changed, only I. The family house is a good twenty-minute walk maybe more to the beaches. My brothers and I would walk or pedal there regularly between repeated attempts to run into each other, for the sport of it all. These days, I had a little rental car handy and would zip down to the village, past the bakery and past the municipal fountain where the women could once be seen beating and cleaning their clothes. I would take the beach road past summer homes now all shuttered for the season. The view of the beach at both high and low tides is magnificent and off in the distance one can see the lighthouse and beyond that the rocky coastline that sweeps around and there the mighty fort sits as it has since the early 14th century waiting for the next invaders or these days more likely a band of international tourists speaking in tongues and armed to the teeth with cameras and iPhones rather than broadswords.

MUSSELS IN WHITE WINE: *MOULES MARINIÈRES*

There has been a simmering feud going on for quite some time. Simmering, I might add, in shallots, onions, country butter and white wine. Our good friends to the north – that would be the Belgians – claim that *moules* done in this fashion has its origins on their soil. They make a strong case to be sure, after all stop in at any little restaurant in Brussels or Antwerp and the *moules* and the *frites* are to die for – almost that is. Move down the

79

coast a bit to Brittany and you will find the Belgian's claim to this dish does not hold up. For Brittany, land of the *moules*, has some of the finest in France perhaps in all the world.

The reason why Breton *Moules Marinières* are so renowned is that this seafood dish is made with cultivated mussels that grow directly on the seabed, on ropes or on stakes – the *bouchots* – in the Bay of Mont-Saint-Michel and in the mouth of the Vilaine river. Such mussels, typical of the Brittany region of France, are quite small, tasty, and fleshy – perfect for the *Moules Marinières* recipe! I can recall back when we first started going to Brittany, at first the seaside resort of Lancieux, I would be on the beach with my friend plucking the *moules* from the rocks and when our buckets were full, we up to the house for lunch.

In Brittany it seems they prepare their *moules* in more ways than Sunday and go to any little restaurant and there is an entire page devoted to *moules*. You may think perhaps I'm a bit one sided with my praises well, you are absolutely right, spot on! There is truly nothing quite like walking over to the seafood establishment (*shhh, not really a "store" if you get my drift, the tax man is none the wiser*) and return home with our *moules*, cut up the onions, per-haps a shallot or two if you wish, a stick of butter, sea salt, coarse black pepper, chopped parsley and thyme, a cup of water and at least one bottle of white wine (I have used two bottles before.). Cover the pot with the lid, decide on your wine, cheese, and ba-guette; then set out a few place mats and large bowls for you and your guests and in no time, you will be reaping an incredibly delicious meal from the Breton waters with a broth that's good enough to have just as a bowl of soup. Now, once small issue that needs to be discussed. How many *moules* per person? As I noted in an earlier story, the wise old country seafood merchant told me her rule of thumb is 1 kg/2.2 lb per person – if it's going to be the main course: and half that if it's an appetizer. To this day, I stick by her rule, thank you Madame, but I will let you all decide. On another note, I suppose it's entirely feasible that one would inquire about the possibility of serving this dish without the wine. My suggestion is that you tell them that all the alcohol is long gone by the time it ever reaches their delicate *bouche*. I refuse to serve it any other way. Merci.

LEG OF LAMB, BRITTANY-STYLE: *GIGOT D'AGNEAU À LA BRETONNE*

*I*f you have ever been to Brittany, you surely know that the region is famous for, among many other things, its lamb – tender, innocent young animals who spend their early years grazing on the salt marshes or meadows off the coast of Brittany and Normandy, coastal areas which are often flooded by the sea in the spring. As a result, the lamb is rich and uniquely flavorful and, in my humble opinion, quite unmatched anywhere. In France, the lambs are slaughtered generally between 120-200 days old. The lamb is served with the traditional garnish of dried white beans. For me, this is a dish that brings back many wonderful memories of family meals at our home in Brittany. Our wonderful cook and housekeeper would present the lamb in all its glory placing in front of my father who would do the honors.

There was actually a translation for the English
who descend on our part of the world

Best French Comfort Foods: Settling in for the Winter

Our thriving metropolis

I suspect the term "Comfort Food" has pretty much the same connotation around the world whether you're in Hanoi, St. Petersburg, Beijing, Cheyenne, WY, or Paree, France. For some, comfort might well mean your Aunt Zelda's chicken soup or Tony's pizza from around the corner, bangers and mash at Ye Olde Pub or an Irish stew, or maybe a plate full of Mom's brownies. All of which sound very tasty I might add. Now in France, they call comfort food *"Cuisine Grand-Mère"* or Grand Mother's cooking and that's an appropriate name, all things being equal. For me, this type of cooking conjures up a special image of a friendly, ruddy-faced country woman with jet black eyes and a quick smile, wearing a blue and white checked apron and decked-out in country slippers or a pair of *sabots* or clogs. It also makes me think of someone who could prepare the most incredibly delicious country meals on the one hand, and on the other perfectly comfortable in field surgery techniques such as slicing a poor duck or chicken's neck or field dressing a rabbit in a minute's time and usually with a large, rather nasty-looking kitchen knife. This is what country living in France was all about! The country's culinary history is steeped in traditions with many a regional dish that has stood the test of time, for centuries.

I learned a lot about French country food, its history and preparation as well as more than one or two country tales. The Bretons are a mystical people in many ways and all one has to do is pick read up on the Arthurian tales. I learned a lot about cuisine not so much from my dear mother who was an excellent cook in her own right having prepared one outstanding French meal after another when we lived in Neuilly. Our country cook in Brittany was a wonderful lady who I have mentioned in many of my stories because she was a part of the Brittany I knew and a part of my growing up. I remember shadowing her movements in the kitchen, cleaning up this or that, chopping one thing or another and most importantly, learning how to get out of her way at critical moments in the cooking process. I would always accompany her to the farm across the road to pick up eggs, fresh milk, and whatever else the farmer might have to sell. Arriving at the farm, I was always speechless. The main room with its rough unfinished floor, and an ever-present smoky wood fire, served as the family's living and dining room and kitchen. In the far corner of the room was a large four-poster bed where the aged grandmother, all wrapped up in her great shawl, presided. The parents and their seven children all slept somewhere upstairs perhaps in the hayloft. I never did find out. This was French farm living circa 1963. In many ways the lifestyle of this particular family and many others like them, at that time, I suspect had not really changed since the 1940's.

The author at a ripe old age of 17

Many of the comfort foods that I have written about in this book had their origins, in one way or another, either from our country kitchen in the Brittany countryside or made their presence known at our dining table in Neuilly s/Seine. I cannot imagine there being a more pronounced difference in settings than between those two worlds. Yet a strong personal connection links them and still remains strong to this day.

Gratineed Chicken in Cream Sauce: *Poulet à la Fermière*

*J*ust when you thought it was safe to finally come out of the hen house!! Thank goodness chickens can't read beyond a third-grade level or I'd be in trouble with this story. To my sheer delight (pretty strong stuff) I re-discovered this dish, thanks to a long rainy weekend and enough time to go through a stack of old *Gourmet* Magazines. I marveled (yes, some people still do that) how such a simple little dish as this could be so incredibly delicious and finger-licking good to boot! Believe it or not if you have kids who think that French is all about, well, French toast and other things, then prove them wrong. Give the little darlings a little taste of French countryside cooking. *D'accord?*

Allow me, your humble servant and culinary *bon-amis*, to provide you with some supplemental information to help round out the dish – add value one might say. If one were to play "purist" the appropriate translation for this dish would be "the farmer's wife's chicken" – and a scared one at that! But the real message that's being conveyed is that *Monsieur le Fermier's* wife cooks with an abundance of fresh ingredients available to her, literally right on the farm. Imagine the concept of "sustainability" but a hundred years ago. I can picture her this very minute, stepping out into the courtyard in her wooden shoes, a few of the smarter chickens would scramble away but eventually would be arrested, drawn, and quartered. Madame would fetch the fresh cream and cheese thanks to their precious cows already out to pasture. Onions, carrots, baby potatoes and peas would all be found in her vegetable garden. If you've spent any time in the French countryside you would know that what I have painted, at one time, was a fairly typical scene. We long to return to those days, it seems, when one could easily draw a line from the farm to the dinner table.

Enjoy this dish, it's great as a Sunday meal or just about any time.

WORLD FAMOUS BICYCLE RACE COMES HOME

This is about a small country village of some 700 inhabitants, tucked peacefully away in Brittany somewhere along that breadth-taking beautiful stretch of coastline known as *la Côte d' Émeraude* or the Emerald Coast. In truth, few things have ever really changed in this part of the world, oh to be sure, many years ago they filmed a swashbuckling-type movie at a nearby castle and indeed a few stars were seen being whisked through town but with that exception, there's been the occasional car accident, usually involving a tourist, some low-level truancy and of course the usual summer tourist falling off the high rocky cliffs. Quite frankly, very little has upset the natural ebb and flow of daily life in this village.

That is, until the day when the mayor proudly announced that their village had been chosen as a *ville de stage* for the Tour de France. It was an event of such seismic proportion and one that would prove to be a life changing moment for everyone.

There are likely few things that truly stir the passion in the French, young and old, as much as the world-famous Tour de France. Years ago, legendary names such as Eddy Merckx, the rivalry between Jacques Anquetil and Raymond Poulidor literally divided France, right down to the smallest village, even families were emotionally split into two rival camps. Today the passions remain as strong, if not stronger, of course with different heroes the likes of Alberto Contador or the Frenchman, Christophe Riblon. For every Frenchman who has a favorite *cycliste*, the Tour de France is an event of passion, high drama, and emotion, discussed at great lengths in cafes or argued in smoky *Bar-Tabac* over beers and endless cigarettes. Although the climax of this exhausting, marathon event culminates on the grand Avenues des Champs-Élysées, the emotional battles are fought tooth-and-nail by brave men, one cycling stage after the next, throughout the French countryside.

Having written an occasional human interest story for my local paper, the editor inquired if I was interested in pedaling over to the *Côtes-d'Armor* in the western part of France and do some sleuthing for a background piece on the upcoming Tour de France. I knew this was an important event near and dear to the hearts and minds of every self-respecting Frenchman. Yet here in the U.S. my impression was that the level of interest was pretty close to where soccer (European football) was some twenty odd years ago. In other words, if football, basketball, or hockey games were on the big screen then why in the world would you want to watch a bike race?

The editor interrupted my deep thoughts, "you speak French, right?" he barked, I assured him I did "well then find out what all this excitements' about, get behind the story, look for the human-interest angle and all the good stuff that goes with it, just don't tell me how to build a bike in the process or strategies to win a bicycle race. I'm in the business of selling newspapers, every living day so don' t forget that." He added "one more thing ace, no four-star hotels or fancy restaurants on my dime. Just come back with a story."

My most unusual assignment took me far from the continental United States to the continent of Europe and France, then six hours overland from Paris to a little village that hugged Brittany's emerald coast. From my research I learned that the village would be hosting a much anticipated and dramatic finish of a "stage" of the Tour de France. The Tour is broken up into twenty-one "stages" located throughout France and each one attracts a large number of followers, tourists, and general sports enthusiasts. Further I learned that the village chosen had a thriving population of approximately 700-year year-around inhabitants, give or take, and an expected uptick during the summer months with the influx of tourists, usually Germans, English or Dutch all arriving on bikes, in campers, cars or just simply hiking.

I was definitely off the beaten path, far from any *route nationale* or for that matter any *route départementale*. I was driving my rented blue Peugeot 307 along the narrow winding roads like some formula race car driver. My French GPS advised me in no uncertain terms that I was exactly five kilometers from my final destination, so I turned off her increasingly annoying voice and enjoyed the last few kilometers in peace. Every so often, at the top of a hill or a bend in the road, I would catch a glimpse of the ocean, a deep emerald blue, I rolled down my window gulping in the fresh sea air that hit me like a ton of bricks; I could almost taste the salt air and I smelt the pungent aroma of a low tide.

Approaching the village limits I slowed to a complete stop as a young woman stood in the middle of the road holding up a home-made stop sign; this was done as she let a dozen or so mud speck-led black, brown, and white cows all heavy with milk emerge from the field and onto to main road. Following the procession was the proud farmer himself wearing a pair of mud-covered rubber boots, a faded blue work shirt, V-neck button sweater, twill pants and a beret pushed down to one side. He looked up at me and from a red flushed face and gave me shy grin and waived politely. As I waited for the bovine procession to clear the road and turn into the farm, I couldn't help but notice a beautiful stone house, type *maison de maitre*, circa late 1800's it seemed with a large fig tree in the courtyard almost covering the white painted shutters on the front of the house which were all still tightly closed for the season. The property had a cozy and inviting look to it and was obviously very well cared for by its owners who were someplace in France or perhaps elsewhere in the world. I drove slowly passed the house trying, unsuccessfully, to get a better look and peering through the immaculately trimmed hedges that surrounded the property. Driving towards the heartbeat of the village, the church circle, I passed a municipal truck parked close to the side of the road and observed two men busily attempting to stretch a banner high above the street that said, "Welcome Tour de France."

It was becoming increasingly clear to me that with the Tour de France six months away, the anticipation was slowly but ever so surely building a head of steam and beginning to permeate the daily ritual of the inhabitants in this "stage" town. Whether it was over a *bol de café* and a *croissant* while reading the sports section in Ouest France or standing in line for a *baguette* at the *Boulangerie-patisserie*, the Tour was becoming the only talk of the town. It was almost as important as the weather!

Madame at the *Boulangerie* told me that the upcoming event was nothing short of a crisis for her and she had no idea how to handle the anticipated volume in *baguettes, demis, couronnes, croissants and patisseries*, she has been having nightmares ever since the announcement, but her doctor has prescribed her a *"calmant"* which she said had helped.

At the *Boucherie-Charcuterie*, Monsieur Daliot appeared to be ahead of the game and had already posted a sign reminding customers to kindly place their special orders well in advance of the event. Monsieur Dalio, in his stained white butchers bib confided in me, as he was busy *ficeler-ing un rôti*, that his customers seemed to have gone, in his words, *un peut fou* with planning special celebrations for the weeks leading up and after the event. He added that he would be hiring a junior butcher from Rennes. One of his customers had informed him that her entire extended family including those from Quimper and Lorient were arriving a month ahead of time with their camping trailers and tents. He shrugged his shoulders and returned to slicing a country ham. End of conversation.

I continued my investigation by going next door to the café bar *Chez Pamplouse* which advertised free *wifi* in large letters on the front door. A song by Pierre Perret was coming from the juke-box, and the jumbo screen had a bike race on from somewhere in North Africa. No other customers seemed to be around. Sitting at the bar I ordered a *petit café* and cognac and bought a *Calva* for Marcel, the owner, who stopped his energetic cleaning the counter just long enough for me to ask him a few questions.

"*Behein oui,* we are all excited to be sure, I mean this event could make my entire *saison d'un seul coup*, so I am very optimistic, I have even invested in a super large flat screen TV."

On the wall near the bar was a picture of a much younger Marcel behind the bar, fitted out in a green and yellow bike jersey holding an armful of flowers and flanked on either side by two blonde beauties.

"So you were a *cycliste* and a champion as well? "I inquired.

Marcel grinned a little embarrassed "That was so many years ago before I hurt myself, you know one bad spill *et voila, on est terminé.*"

The village had one cemetery with a recent expansion, one working farm (down from three some ten years ago), three registered tractors, one movie/celebration combination hall, an elementary school with an undetermined enrollment, a two story, recently refurbished municipal building, and no police station. I wondered about the possible security issues, this being a stage town, how would they handle crowd control and the usual riffraff, bag snatchers, drunks.

The village was served by a local bus which stopped twice daily in front of a *café-bar-tabac*. The village also had a recently elected mayor who, according to the mayor's press office (releases were online no less), had quite an aggressive agenda to promote economic development. I could easily imagine that having a Tour de France stage end in the mayor's back yard was tantamount to an opportunity of a lifetime and one which apparently this mayor, as any other mayor would, fully intended to squeeze out as much political benefit as possible.

From maps it was also evident that central to the village was the church circle so designated because quite simply, the church was there and facing it on one side was a *boulangerie* (a bakery closed on Wednesdays), a *charcuterie* (a butcher shop closed on Wednesdays) and a *cafe-bar-tabac* (yes, closed on Wednesdays). In other words, on Wednesdays, residents of this fine village were simply out of luck, or they drove, bused, or walked to the next village. Outside of the village limits, according to the Guide Michelin, there were three bed and breakfasts, a 15th century fort, and a lighthouse. My goal, my story, was to get a feel for this quaint village before the mad rush of humans descended from around the world and consumed it in the name of the Tour de France.

The *Cap'Coiffure* was open for business and because my locks were getting a bit long, I looked unruly and could easily have been stopped by a *motard* or a *flic* and asked to present my papers. It was also a good way to pick up some information. Madame Stephanie Antoine, who is originally from St. Brieuc, was the proud *patronne* of the establishment which she keeps immaculate, not a hair on the floor anywhere. On this particular morning, her husband Henri had stepped out to buy a copy of Ouest France and a café next door at *Chez Pamplouse*.

I obligingly let her work her magic on me with her scissors. As she snipped her way through my locks, I learned all about the weather and the dampness and the frost and the long-term weather outlook for next week; I also learned that a lady from around the corner had a nasty *crise cardiac* but the ambulance from Erquy had arrived too late. Can you imagine? She confided in me that there was some hanky-panky going on in town involving one of the local shopkeepers, but she wasn't going to say anything more because she wasn't the kind that gossiped. Madame paused as if to catch her breath, I seized the moment and told her there seemed to be quite a sense of excitement in town with the upcoming Stage du Tour de France.

She stopped, put her scissors down, looked at me and said:

"*Mais Monsieur*, let me tell you something: I have been cutting and styling hair for over twenty years now, first in Paris where I received my *certificat* and completed my *stage,* and of course at a *salon de beauté* in Rennes before marrying my husband and coming here. I have never seen so much *euphorie* in my life."

I finished her statement with a question "So, is this a good thing for everyone, for you, for the town, I mean?"

She resumed her clipping

"*Bon, je vais vous dire quelque chose, monsieur, mon mari* Henri and I have already (she lowered her voice at this point) invested in four brand new ergonomic styling chairs, the very latest from Germany which are expected to arrive by train sometime next month and, *de plus*, we are adding a large plasma screen television."

In a triumphant note she added *"Voila Monsieur c'est finis."*

With that said, she spun me around to show off her handy work. The hair cut looked like, well, she seemed so pleased with herself that I paid her, said thank you and left wishing that I had brought along a hat or even a beret.

I wanted to stop at the *Mairie* for a quote or two from the town's newly elected mayor but realized I needed to make an appointment – bureaucracy has no boundaries – so I set one for the following morning before heading back to Paris.

On my way into town, before the bovine experience, I had noticed the *Salons de Crepes*, Café-Bar and decided I would have my dinner there. The menu was pretty straight forward, one could choose from seafood, a variety of pizzas, *galettes* and crepes for dessert. After a glass of *vin de maison*, I started off with the *assiette de saumon fume* which came with lemon and toast points. Being the little food piggy that I am, I had to have a favorite of mine, the *moules Marinières*, the mussels cooked in shallots, white wine, and parsley and my, my, were they ever tasty and succulent. I was not so full that I could not tackle a *galette jambon fromage* which proved to be an excellent choice on my part as their *galettes* were all homemade. For dessert, you will understand, I could not resist having a *crêpe* which is a type of very thin pancake, usually made from wheat flour. The one I chose was filled with melted caramel that's made with the famous salted Breton butter. I concluded there were few things in the world better than that desert. On my way out I noticed they were putting up a jumbo screen in the bar section. They too were planning in anticipation of the coming bike race.

The next morning and sporting a tie for the occasion, I set off for my last interview with Madame *le Maire* who I found seated behind an oversized, sturdy desk working on her laptop busily putting the finishing touches to her speech before the regional agricultural cooperative board on the economic benefits derived from being a *ville d'etape.*

Behind the mayor were pictures of her husband, children, and a few cameo shots of the family, I thought I recognized the Manhattan skyline in one of photos. The desk was flanked on either side by a flag of the *République Française* and one of Brittany. On one wall hung a portrait of the President of the *République* and two smaller photos of the mayor shaking hands with some unidentified government officials and on the other wall was a large aerial view of the village along with a detailed map next to it. The mayor was very cordial, obviously well-educated and would, every so often, slip into English. This was indeed a new breed of mayor.

"The arrival of the Tour de France", the mayor noted leaning forward for emphasis. "In our own backyard is nothing short of miraculous and comes at a time in our village's history when we need it the most. I can tell you in no uncertain terms Monsieur, that my office will do whatever it takes to extract the utmost economic benefit from this blessing; yes, I call it a blessing for that is what it is."

I probed further. "Madame mayor, for example, how are you planning to prepare for this blessed event?"

The mayor sat back in her chair and pondered for a moment.

"Well, for one thing we will be adding a police presence which we plan on having *sur place* at least a month ahead of the event."

I nodded my head thinking smart move mayor, and scribbled furiously "anything else" I asked?

"Yes we are adding a paramedic team thanks to a mutual aid compact with the town of Erquy and of course we are adding 500 hundred portable bathrooms which will be placed along the race course to preserve the delicate coastal ecosystem but there are many other things that the town is doing as well as the cumulative efforts of each and every *petit commerçant*, this is an opportunity of a lifetime Monsieur!"

I didn't know if I was expected to stand, salute or sing the Marseillaise after such a passionate display so we ended up shaking hands and exchanging emails instead.

I had my story all I needed now was to write it for an impatient editor.

A Long Weekend in Brittany

Part 1 – My Journey Begins: Departure from Paris Gare Montparnasse

I am taking full advantage of this nice weather to head to Brittany, La Bretagne, and check on the old family house and maybe, if the spirits doth move me, even take a walk down to the beach by way of the bakery (a reason for everything.) Heading out to Brittany always leaves me with the choice of going via car or SNCF's *Le TGV* that nice super-fast train. I know that slugging it out with every other Frenchman behind the wheel on the *Autoroute de* Normandie will cost me an arm and a leg with the tolls which seem to only escalate in price each year. In the United States, I used to think that driving north to Connecticut from Maryland meant I would have to take out a loan against my house because of the tolls; but that was before I did the *autoroute*. My other option, the TGV, means that I would need to pick-up a rental car, most likely in Rennes, though there is a *location de voiture* – an Avis rental car agency closer to my eventual destination. Sanity and peace of mind ultimately won out and I hailed a cab to the Gare Montparnasse and arrived in time for me to catch the 10:35 TGV to Rennes with one stop at Le Mans – a city known for its famous *Les 24 Heures du Mans* (24 Hours Le Mans car race). That race is considered to be the world's oldest sports car race in endurance racing and held annually since 1923. It's also commonly known as the Grand Prix of Endurance.

The *Gare Montparnasse* is one of six large *terminus* train stations in Paris, located in the XIVe *arrondissement*. This particular station was opened in 1840 and except for a minor mishap when a steam train crashed through the station in 1895 it has been a smooth and well-oiled machine. The Gare and I usually have little or no problems. I get there, pick-up my ticket, grab a quick espresso and a ham and cheese baguette sandwich to go. It can be a little more challenging when you have just landed at De Gaulle and are slightly disoriented. Then, I patiently sit and watch the arrival-departure board as trains arrive and depart. These days it usual to see the machine gun toting paramilitary-types, usually three, walking in a deliberative fashion apart from each but very much together. I am always reminded when I see them of the time in Paris when we would leave school and they would be on the corner, guarding the route the President De Gaulle would be taking. Of course, this was during the French Algerian War and some pretty nasty things were going on in France and in Algeria. So, I have to admit, they did not look any more friendly than those from years back. My advice: when in the train station, it's probably not a good move to jump up and scream "I'm going to Disneyland." In most cases, I find my seat, relax, sleep *et voila*.

Some years ago, I boarded the train to Brittany and presented my ticket to the presiding railroad official who, after giving it a Nano-second glance, looked at me as if I was a complete moron. I had to be from another world, there could be no other conceivable, legitimate excuse.

Monsieur, vous n'avez pas composter votre billet.

Heads turned, quick glances my way then back, passengers next to me looked vaguely embarrassed, and silently thanked God it was not them.

What I had done, quite simply, was once again failed the French State and for that I had thumbed my nose at Napoléon by not having stamped my ticket at one of the many well designated ticket validating machines before boarding the train. The conductor might as well have pointed his finger at me and stated: *J'accuse!!* I was waiting for some French version of Homeland Security, those gentle internal security boys in raincoats and rubber truncheons to haul me off the train and drag me out in front of the crowd, mothers shielding their children's eyes, others suddenly deep in their books or newspapers not wanting to see me being escorted or dragged out of the station. But I, my ham sandwich still clutched in my hand in a death grip, would find myself propelled into some windowless little interrogation room the size of a broom closet with walls decorated with faded, yellowed pictures of Brigitte Bardot along with past railroad villains who had dared to challenge the Republic. I kept wiping my eyes from the overpowering smell of onions, garlic, and dirty socks while anxiously waiting for my interrogators to begin working me over.

But that didn't happen because right then and there I found I could barely speak a word of French. For some reason, it just plain ol' done left me and I played the Ugly American to the hilt and received my Oscar in the shape of a stamped railroad ticket. I could have pleaded eloquently enough in French but ignorance of the law in France equals a firing squad with not even an option of one last bite of baguette before they shoot you. I am not a specialist in *composter* machines and have torn enough tickets in the process, but I grant you this much, when I can't find *une machine* I break out in a sweat and start looking over my shoulder for the ticket squad.

But this time, Lady Luck was looking out for me, and my ticket met the Republic's approval. Another bit of luck, my bags were actually stored above me and not three cars down due to lack of space. We were gliding away from the station, I had a great seat, a spacious area (just me) nice and comfortable, headrest adjusted a bit and getting into the zone. Right about that time, three giant backpacks flew in from somewhere all landing perfectly in the remaining seats; they were followed three mammoth looking pimply faced youths of undetermined ethnic origins (I had thought Nordic but what did I know) who decided they would join me in my peaceful and restful journey westward. They shoved their bags into the overhead and what did not fit very quickly became the fifth passenger. I wasn't sure what they were speaking but it was loud, and they were telling one joke after another followed by loud guffaws and high-fives (now apparently a universal language.) Since they were obviously not French, I played the "American card" and opened Time Magazine which I had planned to read and catch up on their version of the world news. Yes, it worked..."You American, yes?" "Why, yes I am" expressing amazement at his power of deduction "how did you know?" He pointed at the magazine adding "I go soon to New York for school!" The rest, ladies *und* gentleman, is history. Diplomacy can take so many forms.

The conductor's smooth voice announced at Mach 10 speed our arrival into Rennes and of course thanking all of us for riding the TGV and for all to remember (even the Americans) on our next journey to please *composter vos billet s'il vous plait* (well that's what I heard at least.) It never fails that I have all too cleverly saddled myself with an itinerary that has razor sharp time margins. In this case, I could have waited 2hrs for the next train or put myself at the mercy of the TGV effectiveness and efficiency teams to ensure I could make the 15-minute window (like I said, razor sharp). I was lucky this time but, in the past, I have arrived with no second ticket which meant running upstairs and pleading with a very busy ticket master and his *petit pain* that my train was leaving in 10 minutes. I found that pleading my case had the same effect as screaming at him and slowed him down even more. He checked and double checked the departure times from his *horaire,* a book the size of a couple of old Manhattan yellow pages, then wrote out the ticket in painstaking fashion with excellent penmanship I might add, stamping it twice on all three sheets then finally handing me the ticket with a ceremonial *merci monsieur et bonne journée.* With 5 minutes remaining before departure time, I flew towards the train.

The second leg of my journey was not the plush seating of the TGV, but wooden benches, a definite difference. I mean, you could feel it. The train chugged along. More families were on board. A couple of picnic baskets appeared with ruddy faces all around, smiling at each other. It already felt very country, perhaps even from another century, which I am truly thankful for after the hustle bustle of any big city. *En effet,* I was going home. Shortly thereafter, we arrived at our destination. It looked vaguely like a train station, one where you might expect Wyatt Earp and his pearl-handled revolvers, waiting for you and no one else. Or better, an MGM movie scene with a couple of nasty-looking characters in belted raincoats, waiting for you. I could slip out the back, slide under the car and make a run for it. Well, you get the idea. Passengers disembarked and seemed to drift away, somewhere. A couple of sisters greeted each other, one in a black button-up sweater, smock and kitchen slippers, the other in a blue sweater and comfortable, but rough-looking travel shoes. In a measure of increased efficiency, the station management also dealt with car rentals and likely could have booked you a hotel, if you wanted one. Madame saw me and actually recognized me from prior visits. We chatted. I handed her my papers. She stamped them a couple of times, ran my Amex card through, and with a big smile and *"merci, monsieur,"* pointed to her right, where I know there is a little parking lot with a fleet of even smaller rental cars. I walked to my car, a Peugeot 207 made for one small American or several Europeans. I put my one suitcase in the trunk and somehow managed to squeeze myself into the cockpit, being ever so careful of the stick shift.

A LONG WEEKEND IN BRITTANY

Part 2 – The Familiar Road Home

*L*eaving the station and zipping my way through town in my little toy rental car, I head towards the *regionale* road, which is often simply a matter of following one's nose and going around two so-called traffic circles with raised cobblestones, passing a few houses that appear as neat as a pin with their blooming flower boxes, and *voilà,* you've succeeded. When giving directions, I usually tell people to follow the *regionale* because those roads are well-marked. As for me, I make a left turn at the weathered, almost invisible traffic post onto a narrow, two-lane road with enough ups and downs and tight, hairpin turns to keep you awake. In short, everything you would want as you work the stick shift like a race car driver, except for one thing: you're in a matchbox with four wheels with barely enough room to even change your mind. The challenging moments usually come when you have that certain driver on your backside, who somehow feels he can get a better view of the road by moving up then sliding back down and then repeating that until he sees a patch of straightaway and zips past you. We have all been there. I usually greet his passing with a few choice words in French or perhaps even an international digital salute. I noticed that his car plates were not 22, which would have identified the driver as being a local from the *Côtes-d'Armor* in Brittany, which would be acceptable. There was a 75 on his license plate which obviously made it a Parisian and one in a great hurry who could simply not bear behind anyone else. In this region, you're liable to make that sharp turn and come face-to-face with a tractor trailer going at tractor trailer speed with a load of hay. One can opt to get visibly distressed, honk your horn, raise your blood pressure, move up alongside the farmer, or just settle-in and enjoy the lovely view. As kids, we would beg our father to get closer to the trailer, so we could grab some hay. True confession, we would throw the hay at each other and just be wonderful nuisances, until our father swatted one of us. As he would say, "I don't care who did it. It's the first one I can get a hold of." Talk about an injustice!! I should have filed a complaint with the police on the moral grounds that I was "offended." Right!

Finally, you sense you are getting close. We all have that, I think. We're like dogs that smell home and can't seem to get there fast enough. All of sudden, I am the one driving like (excuse me) a mad Parisian behind the wheel. I take one sharp turn after another on two wheels, shaking my fist at the unfortunates (tourists, of course) for getting in my way, playing it fast and easy. And in the process, just being stupid, as well. That is why, instead of following the main road out, I decide to take the challenge road, which hugs the water. It is low tide, and for the most part, it's always that way, but I seem to remember one occasion seeing the water at high tide. The air at low tide has that particularly salty, earthy mucky smell to it. As kids, we would hold our noses, giggle, and point to each other. "You did it! No, you did it!" Until the hand appeared from out of the blue, and we three boys quieted down. I think it's fair to say that at that age, we outdid ourselves in terms of maturity level. The road I chose just happened to be best driven at high speeds in a small car while never once thinking there might be another car around that blind turn.

At long last, you rejoin the main road towards home. It's late afternoon, and all is quiet. No weekend tourists from Germany or elsewhere, looking to camp out. Here and there you see that some houses are all shuttered, patiently waiting for the season to start back up once again and to welcome home their owners. A small roadside sign continues to advertise their excellent goat cheese, which I have yet to try after these many years. A dog barks somewhere because it can. I put the little Peugeot back into first gear and head home.

The village is typical of thousands of other little villages in Brittany, Normandy or wherever else in France with the church commanding center stage on the circle. Around the other side one finds your *boulangerie, patisserie* (bakery), a cafe/bar (also serving as the official bus stop), and just as important, it proclaims proudly that it has Wi-Fi, a *boucherie – charcuterie* (butcher shop*)*, the elementary school and the *Mairie* (city hall) round the rest of this urban zone. If you are looking for the police station, gas station, convenience store, sorry. Well, there was once a convenience store, but because of a certain *affaire de coeur* with another store owner's wife … but I will say no more because I don't gossip. Anyway, that convenience store is closed. Further up the street, if you have a longing for some *moules* (mussels) or *praires* (clams) or a variety of fresh fish, there is a place in someone's garage, and it's only open on certain days of the week at certain hours of the day. If fresh milk and eggs are desired for breakfast, the farmer's wife across the street runs a great little business, and *madame* will be more than glad to accommodate your needs. As a child, I remember going across the street to the old farm to get eggs and a pail of milk. Inside, it could have been a scene out of a French novel or a country painting.

Thinking ahead, I made a stop at the *boulangerie* or bakery and was lucky enough to get one of the last baguettes. Madame does a particularly good business, and there is usually a line waiting outside by the time she opens up in the early morning. *Bonjour, Madame, Monsieur,* and another day starts. I walked over to the *boucherie/ charcuterie* (or the butcher and deli shop) to pick up a few things for dinner. Perhaps some cold cuts, *pâté de campagne* and a *terrine de lapin* (rabbit terrine) caught my eye. Then, much to my horror, I realized I had no wine for dinner and no place to buy it in town. I was at my wits end. I commiserated with *Monsieur le charcutier,* who understood completely my terrible predicament and asked me to wait then returned with two bottles of red wine. Added to the bill, of course. With that, I was on my way home.

A Long Weekend in Brittany

Part 3 – Market Day

$\mathcal{I}$t always strikes me, when I hop a continent or two, how so many things are truly different – usually in a good way and in a way that makes us think less about all that is wrong or could go wrong in the world we left behind some six or 24 hours ago. Our priorities change. We seem to focus on getting to the bakery for that fresh baguette, or making it to the country market, or revisiting the garden for the hundredth time and taking another moment to admire the house, thinking that you actually have found a unique view, a different perspective. You run to get your camera. It never fails to happen each time I'm there. The house stays put. The flowers, many of which my mother had planted years ago, come again each year. The fig tree will inch up and out once more and will continue dropping its figs in the fall onto the old graveled driveway. It will be lovely and warm in the summer, despite the tourists. It will be beautiful in the fall (my favorite time), and it will cold and quite damp in the winter. All that does not change, but what does change is our perspective on things, and it's our moment in life that make us think somehow the house looks different. No, it really does look different.

The following morning, on hearing the sound of cowbells (my very own country alarm clock), I threw off my blankets, which weighed a ton or so it seemed, and pushed open the shutters just in time to see the farmer proudly leading his herd of cows to the neighboring field. I know the farmer. We grew up across the street from each other, veterans of many a fig fight. I took a few seconds to deeply breath-in the country air because it is 100 percent pure, fresh, and powerful, like no other I know. Going to Brittany for the fresh air and its curative properties is completely understand-able in France and quite often recommended.

I decided to stroll down to the bakery, pay my respects to *Madame* and pick-up a baguette and something that was not on my list of healthy foods, an enlarged *pain-au-chocolat,* which I would save for later in the afternoon. Right then, I was content with a couple of the remaining croissants. Things moved fast, and Madame had it figured out almost to the last *baguette and croissant.* They run an efficient operation. One of these days, I want to see the baker, who I know shows up around 3 or 4 in the morning and does his work, leaving the bakery ready to open for business by 7 a.m., if not sooner.

Strolling back to the house, munching a croissant (I could not wait), I nearly got clipped by a local on a motorbike, beret on tightly and the remains of a cigarette glued to his lips. A classic picture, to be sure. He disappeared over the hill. Over my breakfast of croissants, jam, and strong black coffee, I listened to the French news and commentary on the radio. I always had to chuckle because per usual somebody was having another major angst over some socio-political issue that would likely never be resolved. It may have been over the price of milk or affordable education. Grabbing a sweater, even in late May, I decided to drive over to the next town for the weekly event: Market Day.

Market Day is a colorful, fun adventure and one I rarely miss. By the time I parked my little Peugeot half on the sidewalk, as everyone else, the market was already in full gear. The first stall had crates of chickens and little chicks for sale. Though cute, it reminded me of a hundred years ago. We once bought a little duckling as my "pet" until he reached the age of dinner time. Moving past a crowd of locals, merchants, a few tourists with cameras, an occasional lost dog, I stopped at the stand belonging to the cheese lady, a term of art one uses to describe a lady selling cheese. I marveled at the gigantic cheese wheel, almost the size of a tire, which was in front of me. I asked a few polite questions, and I was given the history of French cheese, which concluded with a tasting, of course, and my promise to return for more on my way home.

At last, I spied what I was really looking for. It wasn't that hard because you just had to follow your nose and smell the country sausages cooking. What I needed was *une galette-saucisse Bretonne,* also known as a Breton buckwheat galette, wrapped around a thick country sausage. It is rich, heavy, delicious and a must have! On some things, I can be very traditional, and that pit stop just happens to be one of them. *Galette* in hand, I checked out what was good or new in the market. In addition to the fresh vegetables, seafood, the horse meat stand, cheeses, *charcuterie*, flowers, and a variety of meats all on display, everything is fresher than tomorrow. I did notice that there seemed to be more people selling what they believe are clothes, cheap trinkets and shoes with a high plastic content to them. The only exception to this 1960s Sears catalogue display of clothes are the Breton sweaters (*ah, oui, Monsieur, pure leine*). All wool sweaters, and they itch like the devil! One year, all three brothers were officially dressed in the same sweaters. I couldn't sit still because mine made me itch so much. I finally took it off, but not until the box camera appeared and the photo was snapped.

Leaving the plastic shoes, the berets, and African statues, I gently meandered back, stopping once more at the vegetable stand, choosing something fresh for my dinner, along with a roasting chicken. I returned via the cheese stand and bought a nice, substantial wedge of the cheese that Madame had spent so much time telling me all about. Lastly, I picked up a small Far Breton, really the quintessential flan from Brittany. The best ones are dense, smooth, and studded with rich, Armagnac-soaked prunes. Unimaginably delicious!

That evening, I fell back on an old dinner menu, faithful and easy to prepare: *poulet au thym citronné*. What's even better is that I had all the ingredients I needed, so no improvising because the nearest doctor was in the next village. I had my fat roaster chicken from the market, olive oil, a couple of onions, garlic, and a few lovely and fresh-looking lemons that I also picked up at the market. I had one bottle of red wine left from my friend the butcher. That would have to do (my personal sacrifices have no end!) For the dessert, the famous Far Breton. Time to get to work.

A Long Weekend in Brittany

Part 4 – The Inevitable and Bittersweet Departure

Some years ago, I was on a client assignment in Brussels, a city that I know quite well and enjoy almost as much as I do Antwerp. Prior to my leaving stateside, I had negotiated for a few extra days that allowed me to hop a train to *Paris Nord*, then to the *Gare Montparnasse* and from there to Brittany and the old family home. A perfect spot for some much-needed destressing and relaxation. It all passed so quickly. Four days later, and with a touch of sadness, it was time to draw the shutters closed.

I spent my last afternoon walking through the garden, a leisurely and sentimental stroll from one edge of the property to the other, taking time to sit on the little bench in the far corner and observe, almost secretly, the house from afar. I tried taking in everything that I possibly could. The flowers were still in bloom. The rose bushes were as beautiful as ever, so many planted by my mother long ago. The vegetable garden remained dormant, as it has for so many years now. I recalled pulling potatoes, onions, leeks, string beans and much more as a young boy of seven, under the ever-watchful eye of our dear cook and housekeeper, Simone.

I decided on one last goodbye to my coastline and zipped through town and taking the beach road, just past the bakery on the corner. Long ago, I remember seeing the women pounding their laundry clean on the rocks by the little stream. The beach road had changed considerably with the passage of time and more houses appearing each year, or so it seemed. Before returning home, I took a long look at the beach, the white sand, the emerald green water, the rocky coastline and breathed-in the incredibly fresh sea air. I turned and slowly headed for home.

I made a point of stopping by our neighbor, the farmer who, as I mentioned earlier, I knew since we were kids. A quick "Bonjour" and goodbye, but not before joining he and his wife for *un petit verre*. Over an aperitif, I caught up on local events, and I inquired about his cows. I recalled that his father used to have a name for every one of his 20 or so cows and could proudly recite their names.

When leaving the house, just like when arriving, there are rituals and procedures to follow. One makes sure the house is properly closed down, shutters latched shut, double checking that everything is turned off, floors have been swept, dishes cleaned and put away, refrigerator emptied of remnants from my wild cooking, and trash disposed of.

I closed and locked the back door one last time. A quick glance toward the house and the garden before turning away. My little Peugeot seemed to have been packed with a few more items than when I arrived.

I had a 20-minute drive to catch my train, direct to Paris-Montparnasse with a stop at Le Mans. I would be in Paris by late afternoon. A morning flight, the next day, from de Gaulle International would take me back to Washington.

A Long Weekend in Brittany

Part 5 – Entertaining Reality

When I returned from Brittany and checked my email, I had over 300 vitally important email messages. I turned the computer off.

Why is it that pleasant weekend memories can disappear faster than you can say *salut, mon pote*? The next thing you know, you find yourself back in the mainstream of everyday, urban life with the traffic, Metro and strikes. Your unpleasant landlady miraculously brought back from death's door reminds you about trash day. Wiping your feet before going in the building, you find your news stand no longer carries the *Herald Tribune*. Read *Le Figaro*, Monsieur, and all the many other little things that insist on disturbing your wonderful, post-holiday karma. All sad, but oh so true. On the TGV going back to Paris, I had been doing some thinking about a Yank's perception of a holiday from his side of the pond and those from a European perspective. For example, in most cases I am more than happy to grab a long weekend far away from the madding crowd and without any of my many electronic gadgets that connect me with this century and are determined to intrude into our lives.

I was not about to spend time in the countryside hooked-up and tracked by every cellular phone company in the world, including satellites orbiting and picking vital pieces of intelligence, such as my decision to go with red versus white wine and beef rather than chicken. I can only begin to imagine the vital streams of intel rolling into the screens of analysts of every stripe from every country. "Sir, we found him. He is in the market right now, buying a cut of beef." My decision on beef and red wine would then ultimately be collected, analyzed and assessed to be of strategic culinary value.

Let me clarify something. Some years ago, when I was in Brittany in late September, I took the time to visit the ruins of an old observation tower built by the Knights Templar. Remember, we are talking circa 1100. Templar churches dot the Brittany countryside. That's just one of the many things that I find fascinating with this part of the country. I won't even get into a discussion about the forest of *Brocéliande* which had a reputation in the medieval Europe as a place of magic and mystery. Wrapped into that are the Arthurian legends, all of which held my attention when I was child and to some extent, still do today. There I was absorbing history, thinking about the decades of time that have passed and yet the remains of the tower still stand, admiring the view into the valley. One could see that a storm was developing, slowly rolling in from the sea. Listening closely, you could almost hear the galloping of the knights on horseback, fully expecting them to appear at any moment. Reality intruded when my cell phone rang.

"Hello. This is Ms. Jones from your dentist office. I'm calling to confirm your appointment in two weeks."

My mind switched from knights in shining armor and broad swords to gruesome creatures with dental drills. I did the only self-respecting thing I could do. I threw my phone. It was a good throw if I do say so myself. I know that my phone lies somewhere in the valley, slowly losing its signal and separating me from the modern technological world forever. Could it get any better than that? "We've lost his signal, sir!"

On the other hand, for so many Europeans that I know personally and professionally, the holiday month (either July or an August) is an undeniable fact. It is a shrine one pays homage to. There are no negotiations about taking two and half weeks and "make up the rest in November." No, it is anticipated, planned for, expected, built around. It is as concrete as it gets, it is holy. In fact, there won't even be a strike because that would cut into vacation time. I mean, how serious can you get?

Frankly, my hat is off to each and every one of them. I suppose I am just a bit envious, even though it does stick in my craw because I can't tell you how many times, I have tried to connect with someone for one business reason or another, and I get an automatic reply message that they are away, skiing in the Alps, but looking forward to answering my questions on their return. I hate them for that, I truly do, but I also applaud them as doing the sensible, sane, and right thing. On this side of the pond (that would be the US,) we often live with the tyranny of the boss, the pressure of work, the laptop, and the cell phone, everyone always reachable by text "I know you're on vacation. Company X wants this or that now." We multifunction between eating meals and reading emails. We talk to each other while texting over dinner (excuse me I just have to get this one). Oh, we take our two-week vacation, but we check our email, voice mail, and text messages, because that deal, we're working on that could make or break our year and "our" bonus. Bring your laptop – oh, and the baby, too, I suppose.

I got home from my Brittany vacation and found my mailbox bulging with vital pieces of information, including utility bills, coupons for dog food, medical breakthroughs on skin cleansing creams, and a cream color envelope with my name and address elegantly written out in long hand. It looked strangely like an invitation.

First things first. I have to tackle those three hundred emails. I might have won a contest, and I may not even realize that I am a multi-millionaire. I can throw away all the pots, pans, and junk I have accumulated and retire somewhere with no cell phone. I highlight all my emails and press delete. If it's a crisis, they will come back to me.

The beauty of the Emerald Coast is forever!

Part *II*

MADE IN PARIS

"If you are lucky enough to have lived in Paris as a young man, then wherever you go for the rest of your life, it stays with you, for Paris is a moveable feast."

— *Ernest Hemingway*

The author at age 2 being held by his father. Photo taken in
the apartment on Avenue Victor Hugo, Paris 16e

GROWING UP IN PARIS: BACKGROUND

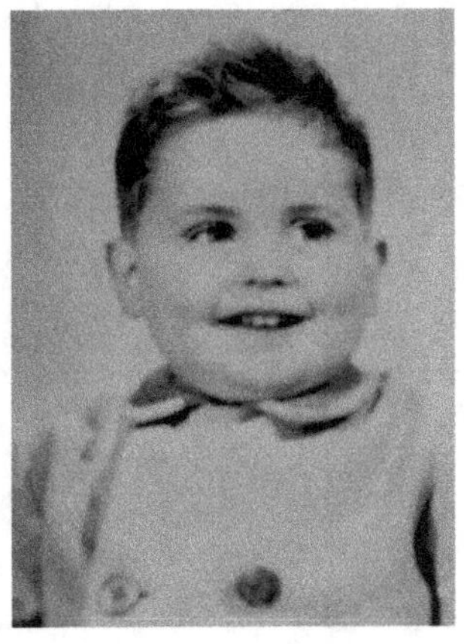

Approach with care. Considered by police to be a well-known, international "Bon Vivant." May be armed with half a baguette. Any information please contact the *Quai des Orfèvres*

They say Paris is unforgettable, and for me that will always be the case. I find my heart aching for Paris especially in the fall when she is, in my opinion, at her very best. Some say Springtime and Paris are synonymous. Perhaps. For me, there is something special about the golden autumn light filtering through the leaves of the mighty Chestnut trees that line the Champs Elysée. The colors are so very evocative and trigger my memories. I experience joy, sadness, and a deep longing for a time that has long past and can never be re-lived. But yes, I was lucky enough to have lived my early boyhood years in Paris and enjoyed my family's spacious home in Neuilly-sur-Seine. Neuilly is a wonderful neighborhood and still very much a desirable, sought-after Parisian suburb within minutes of central Paris. But for me and my two older brothers, I like to think that we lived the Paris life as youngsters at full throttle. We did survive our French school years, and for me, it was by the skin of my teeth, regretting and fighting the system at every moment. We literally ran after the No. 43 bus and hopped on as it was taking off, always immensely pleased with ourselves for our good timing and audacity in making that leap. Pleading forgiveness from the conductor not to be told to get off was, of course, all part of the experience. Challenging "the state" was always a questionable thing to do, but oh so hard to resist!

Yes, I can say we enjoyed our comfortable life. Weekends were spent either sailing our rented boats at Jardin des Tuileries or Luxembourg. On Sunday, without fail, we all managed to be present at the American Cathedral Church on the Avenue George V. It truly is a magnificent church, and inside hung the flags of every U.S. state, on either side of the pews. I returned years later to Paris, and in one of my long walks from the Left Bank over to the Right Bank, I turned up the Avenue George V to the cathedral where we were all baptized. It was as majestic as ever.

On the weekends, my father would often gather up all three boys in order to give my mother some needed quiet time with my sister. At times, we would take our dog to the *Park de St. Cloud,* a beautiful location with acres of land and ample space for our dog to run. Other times, my father would take the three boys to visit one of his old French acquaintances from his OSS war days.

Paris 1950s, very much the way it looked when I was growing up

It was a turbulent political time in Paris with the French administration under General De Gaulle, at odds with those who supported a continuation of French Algeria rather than an independent one. On several occasions, my father would bring my brother's radio into the dining room and place it on the ornate sideboard, next to the silver candelabras (of course,) so that he could listen to the general's radio address. On occasion, my father would slam his hand down on the table in response to one or more particular statements or policy proclamations from the general. At the slamming sound, we all jumped along with the plates and silverware. My dear mother would urge my father to please show some restraint in front of the children.

In support of a continued French Algeria, the *Organisation Armée Secrète* (OAS, or the "Secret Army Organization") was conducting acts of sabotage and assassination in Algeria but also in metropolitan France, including Paris. The OAS was attempting, through terrorism and intimidation, to shape public opinion and prevent Algerian independence. This ultimately led to an ill-fated coup-d'état, to bring down President Charles de Gaulle. For some strange reason, I still can recall the names of the four generals who were complicit in the plot, and I have absolutely no reason why that particular tidbit of useless information has stayed with me.

At school, we students put things into their proper perspective. We referred to the OAS as the *Organisation Anti-Surveillant* (Anti-School Supervisor Organization) or *On a Soif* (We Are Thirsty) there were undoubtedly other variations, some cruder than others, I suspect. Local stores sold packs of little explosives with tiny rocks and some type of gunpowder as I recall, and the little explosives were the size of a Hershey kiss. When thrown against a hard surface they would make a noticeably loud noise. These were somewhat gruesomely referred to, in a sign of the times, as *bombes Algériennes* (Algerian bombs.)

Leaving school each day, I remember on occasion seeing paramilitary soldiers at major intersections all in full camouflage, berets and holding their glistening submachine guns at the ready. For all I know, they may well have been trusted French Foreign Legion paratrooper from nearby barracks. If there were any official cars moving through Paris, then a surprise attack on the general or any of his ministers was entirely feasible. For a short while in Paris, there were checkpoints at night, violent demonstrations, and police stations bombed.

We lived in interesting times.

Le Jardin des Tuileries: Master and Commander

Once, I was a mighty warship captain, navigating the treacherous high seas with a proud and brave crew, ever on the lookout for blood-thirsty pirates trying to destroy my ship. Those were difficult and dangerous times indeed!

Going to the *Jardin des Tuileries* was an outing I eagerly looked forward to. We usually went on the weekends because the beautiful pond with its fountains only gave way to the mighty armadas on the weekends. As a young boy with more than my share of vivid imagination, I was already walking the decks, yelling to the crew to begin preparations for another high seas adventure well before the arrival of the weekend. The more immediate parental threat of possibly missing out on commanding my ship was good enough to make me want to do my homework.

Walking into the *Jardin des Tuileries* from the *Place de la Concorde* was an exciting moment. I would be thinking about who I was going to be that day and what dangerous mission lay ahead. Was I to be an admiral or perhaps a pirate? Would I have a frigate or sloop in the far-off islands, searching for treasure and dodging islanders with deadly blow darts? Not an easy task and not something to be taken lightly. The only dark cloud hanging over this drama would be if the sailboats were all rented. This left you sidelined and watching other captains of the high seas and second guessing their ramming tactics and keeping an eye out for sudden gusts of wind, which were known to send vessels capsizing or even turning upside down. The humiliation from such an event would be almost too much to bear. Not everyone on the high seas were captains. Some were just pleasure sailing, which was fine, as long as they understood that in sailing the high seas, they ran the risk of becoming a target. Before one could say Horatio Hornblower, they would experience ramming speeds, or their sails would become intertwined with another ship. Your casual late afternoon pleasure sail on the Chesapeake Bay could suddenly became your very own nightmare.

There were moments of sheer excitement as your own high-seas vessel made physical contact with another on the high seas. Thanks to the wind, which ruled our destiny, our activities on the water could come to a complete standstill. Not a breath of fresh air to be found, no matter how hard we collectively blew our lungs out in the direction of our sails. We silently prayed for the wind to pick up, looking for a tail-tail to slowly move about, a sail to slowly loft and then it would come rushing in, causing excitement and confusion among the fleet, as our boats spun around, ramming, or being rammed by others. It was an unsettled situation for both captains and their crews. Eventually it happened, as we knew it would, but hoped it never would. The whistle blew. Time was up. Children begged their parents for another round on the high seas. Please, please, I promise this or that. The next line of seafaring captains was already lined up to claim their boat for a high-seas adventure of their own on the pond at the *Jardin des Tuileries.*

Many years later, I returned, thinking surely this activity had long since given way to something more in line with tourist needs. To my surprise, there was the fleet! I sat down in a chair and watched young children eagerly setting their boats in the water, parents yelling out instructions, the usual cutthroat pirate ship heading toward another boat and someone who had no idea what lay in store for them. Boys and girls now made up the admiralty, which was new and different than when I sailed the seas. The sky was getting grey. The wind was slowly picking up. The waves were building. A few drops of rain fell. Tourists scrambled for cover. Mothers and fathers yanked their children from their ships. These high seas were as dangerous as ever. My children, though grown up, had an opportunity to see the fleet firsthand, and who knows, one day they will return, children in hand, and give them an opportunity to sail the high seas.

A SNAPSHOT OF OUR NEUILLY-SUR-SEINE

I must have been looking over some photos that I had taken a while back when I was in Paris. For some reason, It got me thinking about Antwerp, Belgium and the World's Fair in Brussels and our return to Paris. For me, the grand World's Fair was more of a marker, a mental place holder if you will. I admit, I do not recall having visited the World's Fair and the famous Atomium.

One day we were in Elsdonk (a quiet suburb of Antwerp) and the next day in Neuilly, which was Paris. There was no dividing line. It was just greater Paris, greener and cleaner and more expensive. Much later, I learned that Neuilly was a select residential neighborhood, which included many corporate headquarters, a handful of foreign embassies, as well as the well-known American Hospital of Neuilly. It is still one of the wealthiest and most expensive suburbs of Paris, along with the 16th (think Auteuil, Passy, *Bois de Boulogne*) and 7th arrondissements (think the Invalides, Eiffel Tower, and more). All three together are said to form the most affluent and prestigious residential areas in the whole of France. Not entirely sure that I would take that to the bank.

There were a few recognizable names who were among Neuilly's notable residents, including Liliane Bettencourt, L'Oréal heiress and the richest woman in France; Mireille Mathieu, chanson singer; Marine Le Pen; Nicolas Sarkozy, former president of France; the Duke and Duchess of Windsor, who lived at the Villa Windsor; and Edith Piaf, the well-known French singer. There are many more, but I think you get the gist of our shabby Neuilly environment.

Neuilly had a little bit of the best and brightest, including movie stars, writers, film producers, fashion designers, generals, politicians and more. It is also the home of numerous beautiful and graceful looking *hôtels particuliers*. A rough translation might be a private mansion comparable to those comfortable estates in England. In fact, my first school was in Neuilly on the *Avenue du Roule*, and had been, at one time, a *hotel particulier*. The elegant mansion served as the administrative school offices. I have a story to tell, later on, about an American boy, challenging the French state, and his unexpected visit to the headmistress office. He was then and still is, innocent. It was the beginning of several encounters with the French state.

Our apartment was on the rue Perronet, number 61 to be exact. For 1958 standards, the building stuck out like a sore thumb, it was fresh, new, and architecturally quite modern. At that time, recall Paris was just 14 years from having been liberated by the Allied forces. From what I have read about the 1950s, Paris was hardly the lap of luxury, given food shortages, little or no gasoline available, politics in turmoil with the French Communist Party playing an increasing role, much to the dismay of the U.S. For my father, that Paris was his old stomping grounds pre- and post-war.

Our apartment building had four floors. The first, or the *rez-de-chaussée*, was owned (who would challenge) by *Madame la concierge*, who, living up to her noble occupation, knew about everything that was going on in the building. On that same floor were several exceedingly small rooms for those nannies who were attached to residents. The rooms were glorified closets, equipped with a small bathroom. That is where our Lucy lived. My parents had pleaded with Lucy to accompany them from Antwerp, Belgium, her hometown, back to Paris. My sense is that neither my father nor mother wanted to face three unruly children by themselves in Paris. Some months into the arrangement and having had to deal with three choirboys bent on resistance at all costs, Lucy deeply regretted her decision. A year later, she threw in the proverbial towel, exhausted from trying to manage three boys. We had our victory.

There is one architectural element of note about our apartment building that made it unique. It had an underground garage with space for everyone in the building. In all likelihood, given the times, I am going to say there may have been only a few such underground parking facilities attached to apartments in all of greater Paris. Our own apartment was spacious with four nice-sized bedrooms, a large dining area and an equally large living room with a fireplace and a little porch overlooking the gardens below.

That was our home for better or worse until that one morning when we were told that we should plan to say our goodbyes to our schoolteachers and friends. There was no sad *"au revoir"* or hugs from my teacher, I believe mine resented the class interruption and curtly reminded me not to be rude and keep my hands out of pockets. I had almost expected a slap for my insolence, real or not. It was my lucky day, it was my "Get out jail" card. We left one day with just our suitcases and our blue Pan Am bags. The apartment behind us was still fully furnished, my brother's model airplanes still hanging from the ceiling. Everything was the same, just no occupants. Others would handle that little detail.

We flew back to the United States, and three months later, we were in Kinshasa, Democratic Republic of the Congo, deep in the heart of Africa, a new country, just fresh from Belgian independence but still raw with a deep resentment towards their former colonial masters.

THE AMERICAN CATHEDRAL ON AVENUE GEORGE V

oodies worldwide are going to be scratching their heads, trying to grasp the linkage between church and food. Well, besides the obvious that both are good for the soul and more, this subject is something that I have been meaning to write about for a while for a few reasons. The most important one is that I was baptized at the American Cathedral of the Holy Trinity in Paris (The American Cathedral) located at 23, *avenue George V* in the 8th *arrondissement* of Paris. So therefore, everything else must flow from that important marker.

First, a little background. The American Cathedral has a rich history, consecrated on Thanksgiving Day in 1886, but with deeper roots than that, having served the American community in Paris since the 1830s. The present site was purchased on the *Avenue George V* from the estate of the *Duc de Morny,* half-brother of Emperor Napoléon III. The church was built in less than four years. The plans submitted by the English architect George Edmund Street were approved by the vestry in October 1882, and the first services were held in September 1886. What I find very nice is that American decorative touches can be found through-out the cathedral, including needlepoint kneelers, depicting the

50 state flowers and the 50 state flags, which are displayed in the nave. It makes quite an impression! In fact, when I revisited the church, my daughter insisted on having her picture taken underneath the flag of the State of Maryland. Interestingly enough, during the German occupation of France (1940-44), the cathedral was taken over by the German military chaplaincy. The nerve!

The cathedral appears in a wonderful painting titled *Après l'Office à l'Église de la Sainte-Trinité, Noël 1890* ("After the Service at Holy Trinity Church, Christmas 1890") by Jean Béraud. The original painting is on loan to the *Musée Carnavalet* in the 3d *arrondissement* of Paris. It's a beautiful painting, and I missed seeing it in its proper place at the cathedral. Some years ago, I stopped in at the cathedral after an absence of many years and inquired if there would be a way to obtain a copy of my baptismal record. The very kind attendant returned with an oversized, leather-bound ledger: The Register of Baptism 1912 – 1958 and proudly flourished a photocopy of one of the pages with my baptismal record. Our address at that time was listed on the *Avenue Victor Hugo*, Paris 16e. All this was conducted in French, and we parted the best of friends. Madame had clearly understood the importance of what this piece of paper had meant to me.

Reflecting on my years growing up in Paris as a young boy inevitably includes the church services at the American Cathedral. Before moving to *Neuilly*, we lived as I noted earlier, on the *Avenue Victor Hugo*, not that far from the *Avenue George V* and the cathedral. I imagine my grandparents were most likely faithful attendees, as well, when they lived in Paris in the late 1920s and early 1930's residing at their spacious 5th floor apartment on the *Boulevard Suchet* (16e). As for us, every Sunday, we were rounded up from our various hiding places and packed into the old Peugeot 403, leaving my sister behind with the nanny. Out we drove to the *Avenue du Roule* and onto the *Avenue de la Grande Armée*, the *Avenue des Champs-Élysées*, then finally turning onto the *Avenue George V.* More than once, before church services, the then-Rev. Dean Riddle, a veritable fixture in the church in those days, would ask my father if he would read a selection of psalms. It was always impressive for me to see my father standing before the congregation in his dark blue pinstripe suit, knit tie with the ever-present gold tie bar and reading from a lectern with the large gold bald eagle.

The Christmas season brought with it the inevitable question I had hoped and planned to avoid: Was I going to join my brothers and be a good shepherd in this year's pageant? In other words, was I going to wear my dressing gown, a towel over my head, slippers and a staff that looked remarkably like a broom covered in silver wrapping paper? Not on your life! Of course, as it turned out, I reluctantly took my place in line with dressing gown, bedroom slippers and all the paraphernalia of a good shepherd and walked before the entire congregation toward the manger.

Driving back to *Neuilly* after church service, we always looked to see what was playing at the Normandie movie theater, located at the at the intersection of the Avenue George V and the *Champs Élysées*, or further along, the Napoleon theater. This was an opportunity to lay out our plans for the afternoon, how to avoid homework and steal away. We were always scheming. As little angels, crammed in the backseat of our car with yours truly relegated to the middle and each one of us determined to get the other two in trouble with my father, who had a remarkably short fuse. It was a high-stakes game where anyone at any moment could be fingered as the guilty party, and then look out!

The bakeries have fundamentally remained the same
with delicious assortment of pastries.

Stopping at our neighborhood bakery on the *rue de Chezy* just a block from where we lived meant there was actually going to be a real dessert (i.e., the kind we would buy in a bakery) in our near future if we behaved. The threat of any one of us being deprived of a dessert from the bakery was almost too much to bear. One of us would go in the store with either parent, while one always stayed to monitor the two remaining little angels. From the moment the door was pushed open, and the first step taken inside, it was my definition of heaven, clearly and unequivocally. Anyone who knows French bakeries will understand. My nose would press against the glass case, trying to get as close as possible to my version of heaven, eyeing the *Baba au rum*, the *mille feuilles* or *Napoleons*, the chocolate *eclairs* chocolate *eclairs*, *profiteroles* with cream popping out everywhere, *chaussons aux pommes* (delicious oversized apple turnovers), *palmiers*, layers of them all calling out to me, and fruit tarts, little ones and big ones as far as the eye could see. With any luck, we would leave with a couple of *baguettes* and a box of pastries, the contents of which would be revealed only if we finished all our Sunday lunch, and if we behaved at the table, and if we started on our homework, and if we promised to take our baths without a fuss, and if we promised not to fight with each other. Such a deal! We all nodded our heads solemnly in the affirmative. How could anyone not agree to those terms?

I can truthfully say that my mother never once failed to put on a Sunday meal that was anything less than spectacular. It could have been a pork roast, a rare side of roast beef, leg of lamb, veal or pork chops, scalloped potatoes or a *gratin* variety, baby red potatoes, creamed onions, fresh vegetables, endive salad and a wonderful selection of cheeses. And of course, we had our regimen of a little bit of wine mixed with water. It was Sunday. I grew up in a family that favored *Beaujolais, Cotes-du-Rhone, Nuit-St. George* or *St. Emilion* with lunch and dinner. It was just like that. It was my mother who knew her wines and who helped me appreciate them much as she did with opera and classical music. Understanding wines or operas was never on my father's list of interests. Antiques, books, first editions, silverware, paintings, yes for sure. Back to Sunday lunch. Then came dessert, which I thought would never, ever arrive. This time, it was not floating island or lady fingers smothered in sweet cream and liquor, or a *crème brûlée* (oh, not again!) or chocolate mousse. This time, it was the long-awaited box of pastries. We were indeed thankful because this was the real stuff!

As my father would say emphatically, time and time again, taping his finger on the dining room table for emphasis, "Just remember boys, no one cooks better than your mother, and I would dare say it's a darn sight better than what you will find at any one of the finest restaurants in Paris." He would know.

Now you can truly see the linkage between Sunday church and food.

A Most Remarkable Person

*B*efore crossing over the Seine onto the right bank to make my lunch date, I made a quick detour along the *Boulevard Raspaille*, which is in the 7th *arrondissement*, and from there making my way to the *Rue du Bac*. It is an easy, 20-minute walk from my hotel. Once there, it was a walk back in time. I wanted to ponder and share a snapshot of a most remarkable person. I will call her *Tante* Marie. She was not our *Tante* (aunt), but the terminology was useful for children to grasp. Though she died many years ago, I remember her, though vaguely, from my days growing up in Paris. She was an old lady at that time, and I must admit I was always a little bit apprehensive in meeting her. I don't know if I was just afraid of her or curious and afraid.

Operational details on the need for these visits were lost on me, and I suspect, to a large extent, on my brothers, as well. Yet the visits happened with some degree of regularity, usually on a Sunday afternoon, thus leaving my mother to catch her breath and manage my sister, noting that my younger sister was not born until shortly before our departure from Paris. We boys would climb into the old Peugeot, and my father would get behind the wheel, always lighting a cigarette and having his choking fit. Sometimes the cigarette came after the choking fit. We would then drive from Neuilly to the *Rue du Bac* on the Left Bank, which is not a terribly long distance by car. My father always made sure he arrived with fresh cut flowers or a box of chocolates or sometimes both. He was quite the charmer when he wanted to be. One does not arrive empty-handed. That would have been simply bad manners at best. Both gifts were guaranteed favorites and always welcomed by *Tante* Marie. As I said, she lived in on the Rue du Bac in the seventh *arrondissement* just past the *Rue de Grenelle*. She lived in one those classic *Haussmannian*-style buildings that typify Parisian architecture. Above the entrance way to the building was a blue and white ceramic sign, which read "*Gaz à tout les étages*" because it was considered quite something in the late 1880s, to have gas on every floor, and the building owners were more than happy to announce it to the world. To this day, I find that little bit of history quite wonderful.

As I recall, we took the old-style elevator up to her apartment, and the elevator was the kind you might have seen in an old movie where you draw the screen door shut, thus allowing the elevator to climb ever so slowly from one floor to the next. Through the elevator screen, you could look out at the winding marble stairs and the heavily ornate iron and mahogany railing, which followed you up. There was a *minuterie* button, good for a long minute of illumination, sometimes less. Looking back on all of this, it was like being transported back to a 1930s or1940s black-and-white mystery, fully expecting to see Hepburn or Bacall and Bogey walking down the stairs. The ladies so elegant in their furs and Bogey in his classic raincoat and fedora, of course. At a distance, behind them would be two men with their hats pulled down low and wearing full length leather coats. It was made for the movies, except that it was all quite real.

My father knew *Tante* Marie; that was a fact. But the how-when-where, if you will, were always murky. The two would sit and chat over a cup of English tea or a glass of sherry, while we sat reading magazines or our books and trying our best to sit still and not touch or pick something up only to be sternly reminded "children should be seen, not heard." On its face, it was as if my father was just checking up on a dear friend, making sure everything was alright. Move along. Nothing more than that. But there was history there. You could sense it. I do believe that to be true. Much later, I would wonder if they had known each other strictly during the war, or had she known my grandparents in the 1920s and 1930s? It was entirely possible she had even visited my grandparents at their expansive apartment, the entire fifth floor on the *Boulevard Suchet* in the 16th. Perhaps she had been part of an elaborate operation constructed by the allied intelligence services, most likely British, OSS and the French resistance. I leaned in favor of the latter scenario. My father was always tight-lipped about these sorts of things, either because children had no business being nosy, or it was just a matter of long-standing professional practice. It was part of the war, the past and some things were best left alone in the shadows. It was his *métier* talking.

Years later, my father answered my question, but typically always prefacing it with "why in the world do you still want to know about that? It was ages ago." That was more a piece of trade craft, but he answered just the specific question (and not a crumb more!), so you had to be sure your question got to the meat of the issue. In any event, my father told us that this frail lady had been part of the French Resistance, participating in hiding and sheltering allied pilots who had parachuted somewhere over Europe and were now attempting to make their way across, attempting to reach England via the underground. *Tante* Marie was one of many brave souls who decided they would risk their livers by resisting and hiding allied pilots in their homes and in doing so contributing to winning the war and saving pilots who were critical to the war effort. Many paid with their lives before a firing squad or were deported to death camps in Germany. The French underground would move the fliers from location to location, gradually making their way down south via Bordeaux or Toulouse, then from there over mountains through Spain, Portugal, Gibraltar and finally England. Supposedly, the first American flier downed over France and who used the Underground Railroad was in 1943. It's something to ponder at the courage of one's convictions to take part in hiding allied troops in the middle of Paris, under the ever-watchful eyes of neighborhood spies and the *Abwehr,* the German military intelligence, which had eyes and ears everywhere, as well as the dreaded Gestapo. The level of scrutiny by the Germans rose to a fever pitch as the Allied air attacks increased in 1943 and 1944, yet still *Tante* Marie and many others like her continued their work in hiding Allied fliers, not only Americans, but English, Polish, Canadians, and others, as well. It was her war and one which she played out in the shadows of Paris, a very deadly game of cat and mouse.

Nothing is ever truly buried, and the search to understand certain events during those times and my father's relationship before, during or after the war still remains in large part a mystery and will remain forever well-hidden.

Isadora Duncan and the Last Social Season in Paris

When my paternal grandmother arrived in Paris in the spring of 1913, she was 23 years old. She and her aunt and uncle went to see Isadora Duncan, the first modern dancer on stage. Isadora was then taking all of Parisian society by storm.

My grandmother had arrived with two of her friends from Cincinnati, both of whom had married into the European aristocracy, one becoming the Princess Lea and the other the Princess Louis. My grandmother spent that autumn and winter of 1913-1914 with them in Paris at their apartment in the 16th on the corner of the *Rue de Lubeckand* and the *Rue de Magdebourg*, near the *Trocadero*. It was through them that she was introduced, as my father later noted, "into the best that pre-war Parisian society had to offer, which was considerable. She was then 23 years old, highly impressionable, and exceptionally beautiful."

Very soon, she had a string of admirers whose pleasure it was to ensure that she missed nothing of the full flavor of what was to be the last pre-war Paris season. Again, according to my father's records, "among other excitements, she was presented to a Russian Grand Duchess and saw Bernhardt in *Phedre*. One of her most persistent suitors was the young Marquis Antoine de Gharrette, who desperately wanted to marry her, but at that stage she was not yet conditioned to the idea of marrying a foreigner and living abroad, and she refused him.

In the late spring of 1914, my grandmother returned to the United States, making the crossing on the ill-fated Lusitania.

But back to Isadora.

In 1927, Isadora Duncan, was killed outside her hotel in what can only be described as a freak accident. Isadora was at beautiful Hotel *Le Negresco* in Nice, France. When her car took off, her long red scarf that was draped around her neck flew out in the wind and into the well of the rear wheel. Unaware, the chauffeur of the sports car continued forward with the scarf winding around the axle and tightening like a vice around Isadora's neck and dragging her up from the open car onto the cobblestone streets. She died instantly. The papers reported at the time that she was "jerked from her auto by a scarf about her neck." Bizarre?

Hotel Le Negresco, Nice, France

In April 1913, Duncan's two children, Patrick, 6, and Deirdre, the baby, went for a drive with their governess in Paris. The car's brakes failed to hold while approaching the Seine, and the car plunged into the river. The children and the governess were drowned. Unusual?

THE VICE CONSUL OR A SECRET EXCHANGE IN *AUTEUIL*

The more identities a man has, the more they express the
person they conceal."
> — John le Carré, *Tinker, Tailor, Soldier, Spy*

*P*aris in 1948. It was going to be a lovely late fall day, the
kind that brought out the very best in the City of Light.
The mighty chestnut trees lining the broad avenues and the grand
boulevards were proudly showing off their fall foliage, hinting

that winter's approach might just be around the corner. With the morning chill, one found that a smart tweed jacket or perhaps a light sweater was indeed the perfect companion. By midday, the gentle warmth of an autumnal sun could almost fool you into believing that it was spring that was around the corner, not winter. It felt good just to be in Paris.

The well-dressed man made his way through the heavy wrought-iron front gates of the American Embassy at *4 avenue Gabriel.* The Marine guard snapped at attention as he passed. Indeed, the man worked at the embassy and did hold the official title of Vice-Consul, American Embassy, Paris. Those facts were quite indisputable and quite true; however, any other similarities with his actual duties and those of the Consular Service dead-ended there. His work behind the walls of the embassy were quite different to say the least as he certainly did not concern himself with visas, lost passports, stranded Americans, or those who found themselves at odds with the French police. To a certain extent, it could be said that his work was really more of a continuation of his wartime service and more often than not with many of the same men and women who had been part of that Oh-So-Social club. But now with the onset of the Cold War, the political terrain had clearly changed. Old war enemies were now friends, and there were some allies that are not trusted today. The game had become more complex with even greater ambiguity than ever before. The only constant was that it remained quite deadly.

The American was in his mid-thirties, of medium build and height, with curly black hair and a receding hairline. He would not necessarily be expected to stand out in a crowd as someone who was an American and glaringly so. If anything, one would have thought he was just another European, French most likely or perhaps Swiss. His command of the French language was second to none and could easily have had any French person believing he was who he said he was. The American was well dressed that morning, but in that understated, prep-school, Ivy manner that spoke volumes to the well-trained eye. A muted tweed jacket (tailored by *Gardiner and Woolley*, London SW1), a silk, cream-colored pocket square, a white linen shirt, collar bar and regimental tie, grey flannels with a perfect crease and cuffs that barely covered his argyle socks and highly polished loafers, the pennies left out. The American glanced at his elegant, paper-thin Cartier tank watch. It was almost noon. He hurried to the Metro and within minutes was at the George V stop and from there only a short walk home to the apartment at 11 *avenue Victor Hugo*. He made a quick stop at their local *boulangerie patisserie "Oui, merci,"* he answered the bubbly *serveuse* behind the counter. His wife was resting, but otherwise feeling fine. She had taken an immediate and intense interest in his wife's condition and was always full of homespun advice. Getting her to the country for some good fresh air seemed to be her favorite remedy. In point of fact, it was her only remedy. It was always something to do with the mystical powers in "the air."

The American enjoyed being home for lunch, especially now with his wife, who was expecting their first child. Their apartment was in a stately, Haussmanian-style building with a pair of giant double doors and extensive, ornate iron work on each of the balconies above. The couple lived on the fourth floor, apartment 4-B to be exact. He closed the grated cage door shut as the elevator, most likely circa 1930s, jerked up and began its painful rise, creaking and groaning as it slowly moved up to the fourth floor. Their apartment was elegantly furnished with a tasteful assortment of French and English antiques, many of which had belonged to his parents when they lived in fashionable *Auteuil* in the 1920s and 1930s. A large Persian rug in muted colors covered the living room, and a well-worn, but smaller, Chinese rug covered the floor in the dining area. Over the fireplace hung an ornate, framed painting of his mother as a young lady circa 1914 just before her visit to Paris in time for the last fall social season before the war. She would see Sarah Bernhardt on stage. Bookshelves, floor to ceiling, framed either side of the windows and were filled with any number of first editions in beautiful leather binding. There would never ever be enough room for all his books. He kissed his wife ever so gently, noticing that she seemed pale and in his humble opinion had not fully recovered from her mother's extended visit. He had personally given his mother-in-law the gold-plated tour of the Paris he loved and knew so well. He presented his wife with a box of *marrons glacés* (glazed chestnuts) from their favorite *patisserie,* hoping it would bring smile, and indeed it did. As for him, he found those things far too sweet to his liking. Their *femme de ménage*, Amélie, announced that lunch was ready. The housemaid had prepared a simple, but tasty, meal of cold roast beef, roasted potatoes, green salad and a cheese plate. After a glass of Beaujolais, two *demi-tasse*, and endless cigarettes, he left. A kiss, *à bientôt, ma chérie,* and he was gone. She would stand by the door and listen to the elevator creaking and groaning as it made its way down to the *rez-de-chaussez,* straining her ear to hear his footsteps and then the sound of the massive front door slamming shut.

Out on the avenue Victor Hugo, the American easily waved down a taxi and got in, "*direction l'Eglise d'Auteuil.*" He looked at his watch. He had plenty of time before the *rendez-vous*. He ran through his mind once again the file on André Valient, real name Dimitri Vasilievich, code name "Lambert." Dimitri occupied the post of special assistant to the Acting Secretary General of the *Parti Communiste Français,* better known as the PCF or the French Communist Party. Dimitri was born of a Russian father and French mother. Before the Second World War, he had served in one of the International Brigades sent to Spain to fight against Franco. In France, the father had served in a liaison capacity with one of the many French communist resistance splinter groups, who claimed that only they carried the true mantle of Soviet socialism. After the war, Dimitri's father, by then well along in his years, at the invitation of the Party, returned to Moscow as a hero of the Soviet state. He was subsequently tried on unspecified crimes against the party and the Soviet state, found guilty and summarily shot. Dimitri had been approached shortly thereafter and carefully and methodically befriended by the Americans who offered him an opportunity to channel the bitterness and anger he felt toward the Soviets. In this business, it was a classic, tried-and-true move. Dimitri rapidly became one their best sources of information on the PCF, as well as giving insight on the inner workings, political infighting and leadership. This was especially important, as the Americans were working to support non-revolutionary communists in France and offset an-ever growing Soviet influence on the more radical elements in the PCF.

One thing was clear to the American, and for that matter most of his colleagues at the Paris station: that as an asset, Lambert was for the moment invaluable, and the required caring and feeding to nurture him along was just part of the business of working an asset, any asset for that matter. It was trade craft 101.

You befriended them, became their confidant. You shared in their happiness and comforted them in their moments sorrow, and you reassured them in their moments of uncertainty and doubt, which was often. Yes, you worked them, urged them along, lectured them or used the carrot-and-stick approach when necessary. Then one day, they outlived their usefulness, and the strings were cut. If they were compromised, you cut your losses, realizing they would meet a sure and certain fate. The American knew this all too well. It was a cold, hard fact, and it was a reality. He had run agents and set up networks in Paris during and after the war. He had won some and lost some. It was the nature of the business. These days, it wasn't always the Soviets that bothered him, but the French intelligence service, or the *Direction de la Surveillance du Territoire* (*Directorate of Territorial Surveillance*), that more often than not was the source of his frustrations. They were fair-weather friends and allies who enjoyed playing both sides of the fence and were remarkably good at it. They would share lunch with you one day, and the next they traded information on one of your assets to the Russian intelligence service in return for information. Trust, in this business, was always a commodity in short supply, and it seemed only more so these days.

The American pointed to the *Eglise* and asked the driver to stop in front. He waited a moment then entered the church and exited by the side door. He strolled to the news kiosk and paid for a copy of *Le Monde*, a relative newcomer to the cut-throat newspaper business, but rapidly becoming the preferred daily of French intellectuals, civil servants and academics, particularly those in the higher echelons. Within minutes, the American was descending the steps to the metro, and two stops later he got off at

Porte d'Auteuil. Once more, he took his time, stopping occasionally and giving the impression of carefully inspecting a storefront window. The American liked *Auteuil* for the simple reason that it brought back memories of his Paris days when he was a young student. The area is considered as one of the richest in Paris, with calm, select and expensive neighborhoods, including any number of mansions. Recalling his French schooling, he knew that the village dated back to somewhere between the 13th and 17th centuries and had once been a fashionable country retreat for the French elite during the reign of Louis XV. *Auteuil,* once home to Victor Hugo and *Molière* and the birthplace of Marcel Proust, had been incorporated into the city of Paris around 1860. The American walked along the boulevard until he reached a specific park bench and sat down while carefully placing the folded newspaper to his right side. He waited. With his back to the *Bois de Boulogne,* he surveyed the grand buildings along the boulevard, but the one that he inevitably returned to was *43 boulevard Suchet.* He recalled that the building had been designed in 1925 by the then well-known architect Charles Labro.

The American looked at his watch and waited. He lit a cigarette and stared at number 43. He thought to himself, "Auteuil 12-06." He knew that number by heart, just as he would always remember his dog tag number. For just a moment, he allowed himself to go back to another time. He watched the front door of the building swing open wide as two young boys charged out, swinging their book bags at each other, having an imaginary sword fight and running down the boulevard and to the school. The other boy was Fred, his very best of friend, who lived on the third floor, while he was two floors up on the fifth. He could visualize everything, almost as if it were yesterday. One of the family's gleaming Rolls Royce's pulling up to the curb as he watched Pierre, their chauffeur, swiftly coming around and opening the back door, holding it ready as mother, elegant and dressed in her finest, would be followed by Papa in a somber three-piece banker's suit, hat and gloves, forever checking his gold pocket watch, mindful of the stock market's opening bell on Wall Street. "How would the market open today? Would the stock market continue to slide or was the worst over?" he wondered to himself almost daily. The market would never recover in time, the American thought to himself. Never in time. The course of world financial events would change their lives forever.

He recalled who had lived on the second floor. The husband was Swiss, and his wife was English. They always seemed to have plenty of money. He clearly remembered the time they all went in the car to the *Theatre du Chatelet* for "*L'Auberge du Cheval Blanc.*" They were going to celebrate his sister's birthday but were involved in a car accident in the Place de l'Alma, and his mother had broken her pelvis. They had spent that evening at the American Hospital in Neuilly. On the sixth floor of their building, directly above his parents' apartment, lived a well-known couple who had made their fortune in the perfume business. She and her husband were the geniuses behind the *maison de parfum's* spectacular success. They were always treated very much like royalty. Not to be bothered or approached for anything. When he returned to Paris in 1947, he was invited to their apartment for dinner. They had moved from the sixth and now occupied his parents' floor on the fifth. It was very strange indeed.

The man sat down on the bench and turned to the American, asking, "Please excuse me, but have you finished with your newspaper?" The question was asked in French apologetically. The American moved the newspaper, now holding a bulging envelope hidden in the fold, in the man's direction. The envelope promptly disappeared inside the man's overcoat. He stared straight ahead and spoke carefully, deliberately, as if to make sure the American heard and absorbed everything he said and thus was able to commit it to memory. Less than 15 minutes later, Dimitri got up and crossed into the *Bois de Boulogne* and disappeared. The American lit another cigarette, waited until he had finished smoking then walked up the *Boulevard Suchet.* He would catch a metro at the *Port d'Auteuil,* then a cab to the American Embassy, *4 avenue Gabriel.*

He looked at his watch. He remembered they were having friends over for cocktails that evening. He'd pick up a bottle of Scotch on the way home.

"Never trade a secret. You'll always get the short end of the bargain."

— John le Carré, *The Mission Song*

A Passing Glimpse of Paris, circa 1926

I noted in the previous story about my paternal grandmother arriving in Paris in 1913 in time for the last big social season and before the guns of August 1914 were heard across Europe.

My father and his parents arrived in Paris in the spring of 1926 and shortly thereafter moved into the entire fifth floor at 33, *Boulevard Suchet*, Paris 16e. According to my father, "The building was built by Charles Labro, architect, in 1925. There were six floors and one apartment to each floor plus a small garden apartment on the ground floor, and the seventh floor was reserved for the servants. We had three. The concierge's quarters were also on the ground floor, as usual."

"The sixth floor (the one above my grandparents) was occupied by a very rich, childless couple. Their money came from Parfums Caron, and when I was summoned to the apartment after the war, in the 1950s during the occupation, along with many very rich people, they refugeed to a suite in the Ritz," my father said. "Your mother and I had dinner with them on one occasion in1947, and they always sent her a selection of perfumes at Christmas. We had nothing to do with them while we lived in the boulevard Suchet. Even in the elevator, we didn't go beyond the fifth floor. The concierge was always referring to them as the deity."

"There was a cramped back staircase with a servant's toilet on each floor, as well as a back door to each kitchen and a side door to each apartment. The front stairs wound majestically upwards, with a fine *fer forge* or wrought iron and blue carpet with a border of oak leaves," my father said. "The stairs were white stone, and there was a series of windows with stained glass borders all the way up. The elevator, frequently *en panne* or out-of-service, held two persons at the most. I carved my initials on one of the panels with the door key. They were still there when I went back after the war."

Again, from my father's recollections: "There were two cellars, one for firewood and storage, and one a wine cellar. I remember Papa's concern to put it mildly when his stock of champagne was found to be flat! The courtyard was lined with garages of which ours was the centerpiece and the largest. When I last saw the courtyard, it had not changed at all. At one time, we even had two garages, one for Papa's blue Chrysler (with rumble seat) and one for the majestic Rolls Royce, chauffeur-driven and mostly used by Mother and Grandmother. We had several chauffeurs over the years."

SNAPSHOTS OF GROWING UP
IN NEUILLY-SUR-SEINE

An American Trilogy: Part 1 of 3

I grew up in *Neuilly-sur-Seine* just outside of Paris. In the first of this trilogy, I paint a general background filling in some additional information about life in Neuilly, a little bit more about this special location, our apartment, and our neighborhood. The second part is a about what can happen when three boys put their clever little heads together — perhaps a second revolution? The last part is a case of civil disobedience, yours truly versus the French school system over a mere infraction. I recount my circular conversations, much later as an adult, with officials from the local *mairie* (city hall). Some things just do not change.

Some years ago, in the fashionable suburbs of Paris known as *Neuilly-sur-Seine,* there lived an American family: father, mother, three boys, two girls and one cocker spaniel. For those of you who may not be that familiar with *Neuilly,* geographically it lies to the west of Paris and is approximately four miles away from the heart of Paris. It is a seamless transition from the *Ville de Paris* to *Neuilly.* One broad, leafy avenue leads into another, and you're there. Ever since the early 1900s, Neuilly has been made up of mostly wealthy, select residential neighborhoods, including the headquarters of several corporations. It is often lumped together with some areas of the neighboring 16th *arrondissement* of Paris, marked as Auteuil-Neuilly-Passy, a compendium of upscale neighborhoods. Both Auteuil and Passy were once independent jurisdictions that were just too juicy a target for the City of Paris not to want to incorporate them. While the City of Paris tried several times to incorporate Neuilly, they were never successful. Two items that are worthy of note: One of Neuilly's famous residents was a gentleman by the name of Nicolas Sarkozy, president of France since 2007, and mayor of Neuilly-sur-Seine from 1983 to 2002. Second is the famous American Hospital of Paris, which is also located in Neuilly at 63 *boulevard Victor Hugo.* I touched briefly on the hospital in earlier stories, but note that all my siblings, except for one, made their world-famous debut at that hospital. My other sibling was born deep in the heart of the Confederacy in Wilmington, North Carolina (more family stories there than you can shake a stick at!) In any event, the American Hospital is steeped in history, and if you have the time, pick up a copy of "Americans in Paris" by Charles Glass. That book touches on this topic quite nicely.

When my father was growing up in Paris in the late 1920s and early 1930s in Auteuil on the *Boulevard Suchet* (16th *arrondissement*), the father of one of his chums was a noted administrator at the well-known American Hospital in Neuilly. My father and his friend were boyhood chums and first met in *Le Touquet,* where both families would spend the lazy summer days with their staff of chauffeurs, nannies, cooks and more taking care of all their needs. For purposes of symmetry only, just around the same time, my mother's family could be found loung-ing on the beach or strolling along the boardwalk in Cannes on the Côte d'Azur. At that time, *Le Touquet* was quite the place to see and be seen and was known as "Paris by the sea" with a reputation as being the most elegant holiday resort of northern France, the playground of rich Parisians. Some 30 years later and about as far from Neuilly as possibly imaginable, my father met up with his old friend from Neuilly/*Le Touquet* in a post-colonial country, somewhere in the deepest heart of Africa. Now that is what I would call a well-researched dossier. Hardly circumstan-tial, need I say more.

American Hospital of Neuilly, 2011

Photo attributed to: Siren-Com. Own work

We lived on the *rue* Perronet (named after *Jean-Rodolph Perronet,* an 18th century French architect and engineer and best known for his work on the *Pont de la Concorde.*) *Rue* Perronet was a quiet side street located just off the *Boulevard d'Inkermann,* which led you to the Avenue *du Roule,* one of Neuilly's principal thoroughfares, which ran parallel to the Avenue Charles De Gaulle (formerly Avenue de Neuilly.) I will not go into too much detail about our apartment other than to say it was on the second floor, and as I remember, it was extremely well-furnished with both English and French antiques, beautiful Persian rugs and several nicely framed paintings and portraits. I know several pieces were from my grandparent's apartment on the *Boulevard Suchet,* but there were also several pieces that my father had cleverly unearthed in one antique store or another. It was his passion, and he was extremely knowledgeable about certain items of interest, such as French and English antiques, antique clocks, English and French silverware, signed drawings, first editions. In retrospect, he would have been better as an antique dealer for a company such as Sotheby's. I believe he missed his real professional occupation.

In this spacious apartment, there were four nice-sized bedrooms, a day room/nursery, a large dining room area where we would all gather *en famille* for lunch and dinner, a kitchen and a living room with a fireplace and a small balcony, which overlooked the gardens. Our bedrooms faced out onto the *rue Perronet,* and each bedroom had its own balcony, which for us proved to be invaluable as a launching platform for some of our guerrilla activities. Our Belgian nanny, as you may recall, lived on the first floor. The nanny was hardly the benevolent Mary Poppins kind, and I grudgingly imagine that her sturdy Flemish character was necessary to manage three boys. She would take me for walks along the *Avenue du Roule* and would slow down just in front of the *gendarmerie*, the police station, and remind me that all I had to do was step out of line, and she would take me there personally. The station guard looked tough, casually holding his submachine gun ever at the ready. I never really thought the threat through, or I would have had a severe case of civil disobedience. I should note that all nannies were within earshot of the *concierge*, Madame Busybody, the self-appointed keeper of French civility, law and order. She had a better sense of who was doing what to whom and when than most Secret Service and the FBI combined. It was easier to get past a tough Homeland Security customs officer, than it would have been slipping past Madame Busybody.

Across the street from the apartment was the *Lycée Pasteur*, a well-known boy's school. The school had been scheduled to open its doors for the first time in October 1914, but instead the government requisitioned it as a field hospital for the duration of the war, 1914-18. School session began in 1923 and has been going strong ever since. My reason for mentioning that little factoid is that while it might have made sense for the three boys to go to school there, next door, the rationale for us attending the *École Pascal* in Paris, in the 16th arrondissement on *boulevard Lannes* made more sense because my father had been a student there. With unquestionable logic, if it had been good for him then, it should be equally as good for us now. Case closed. There were times when one could hear the schoolboys at *Lycée Pasteur*, and every so often the sound of a professor yelling at some poor student, which undoubtedly would be followed by a well-aimed eraser or piece of chalk or whatever else was handy. We had the same

French instructional system. Those gentle reminders were designed to help build character. There was a professor in attendance at that time, and had I only known I would have brushed up on my existential philosophy. Jean Paul Sartre taught philosophy at the *Lycée* for several years, sharing his view of the world while at the same time thinking of meeting someone for a late afternoon appointment, perhaps with *Le Castor (Simone de Beauvoir.)*

Further along on our little *quartier* on the *rue Perronet* and walking toward the *rue de Chezy* was our corner grocery store with all the typical fresh produce, all colorfully displayed outside. My mother would dutifully grocery shop on a daily basis and would walk to the greengrocer and from there across the street to the *boucherie-charcuterie (et chevalinne)* (the butcher and deli shop) with the unmistakable sign of a horsehead out in front. Once the roast was purchased and put in the *filet* or knit grocery bag, then it was just a matter of walking a few more feet to the bakery for a baguette or two. By then, the shopping essentials for the day or the next few days were complete. On the *rue de Chezy* was the *Chezy* movie theater, our lifeblood, and as kids we would always take time to stop and look at the coming attractions. Sometimes we lingered a little longer, if there was a Roman centurion sword against sword with Kirk Douglas in a gladiator scene, or better yet some scantily clad mademoiselle starring in a detective movie with Jean Gabin.

Some years ago, when I returned to our little *quartier*, the corner store had vanished, giving way to some faceless *bureau* of some sort. The butcher shop was also gone, but the *charcuterie* was there with the ever-present tasteful window assortment of pig's feet or snout arranged in aspic, *pâté, andouille* sausage, black pudding, *rillettes*, hams, headcheese, and heaping piles of sauerkraut or *choucroute garnie.* I will admit it did not look as nearly as appetizing then as it looked now. But I said a prayer of gratitude that the *boulangerie*, our bakery, was there. I had to do what any self-respecting person would do. I went to take it all in. The elegant visual display of the *patisseries*, the line-up of *baguettes, couronnes, pain demi,* and the delicious aromas that come with any French bakery. Ever mindful of the importance of politeness, and since it was in the afternoon, I purchased a *petit pain au chocolat* and a *chaussons-aux-pommes* just in case I felt faint from hunger.

The author's father, Paris 1952

An American Trilogy: Part 2 of 3

The *rue Perronet,* where our apartment was located, was sometimes referred to as *la séduisante rue Perronet,* though "seductive" still eludes me. We were just a couple of miles from the *Arc de Triomphe* and only a few minutes by bus on the No. 43 to the *Place des Ternes,* which straddles the 8th and 17th *arrondissements.* More often than not, we would be running late for school and would race up to the *Avenue du Roule* and catch the 43 bus and changing at *Place* des *Ternes* to another bus that would then take us to *Boulevard Lannes.* Most of the time, it was great fun running to catch up to the bus, then jumping aboard before the conductor signaled the driver to take off. Sometimes the bus was already on its way, and one had to jump on by holding the rail. Such excitement, but how we survived and did not get run over or injured in some fashion remains a mystery. God works in mysterious ways. Looking back, I am sure that it took everything my parents had and more to try and keep the lid on three spirited, rebellious, and curious young lads. The next part of the story is an example of what can happen when you leave three boys unsupervised for too long. (My grandchildren have yet to hear this story, and I'm saving it for the right time.)

There were any number of antics that would put my father right on the edge of completely losing it, as they say. In fact, it was that spot we all watched and waited, both in fear and fascination. One time we pushed the envelope of mischief. As I noted earlier, our three bedrooms faced the street and we all had access to a balcony, which ran the length of the apartment, but only my room had the sliding door to reach the balcony. By way of a quick historical backdrop, the issue *du jour* that grabbed every one's attention, even little *écolier* students like us, was the Algerian question which I have already made mention of. Throughout Paris, there was a certain sense of high alert, as there were any number of *manifestations* or strikes and solidarity marches for one side or the other. If you are familiar with the book/movie "The Day of the Jackal," that should put the events into some context for you, but I would recommend a far better read: "A Savage War of Peace." Three innocent little American boys had procured a supply of projectiles known then as *bombes Algeriennes* or Algerian bombs. I am not totally sure how we obtained our supplies, but most school kids seemed to have had their own personal stash and I suspect there had to have been an active trading scheme for these projectiles. The projectiles when thrown against the pavement or car would explode with a very nice, loud bang.

It was a quiet Saturday afternoon when the special operations team put their plan into action. For a while we amused ourselves and worked on perfecting our aim by throwing the bombs in front of unsuspecting elderly people (that meant anyone above

30, most likely) who were usually carrying grocery bags and making their way down *rue Perronet* unaware of teenage ninjas. The result, predictably and dearly hoped for, would be a strong reaction, a scream, shaking a fist at someone, then looking around for the culprits, who by then were out of sight, shielded by the balcony wall. Our attacks were quick and efficient, and I like to think that the successful, surgical military strikes we read about today were copied in large part from our early street tactics. Not at all inconceivable.

All good things must come to an end, or at least must come to an end when you narrowly miss death or dinner for a year. The operational group (all members had a *nom de guerre*) decided that based on our success metrics, numbers of grocery bags dropped, bottles of milk broken, falls on the sidewalk, runaway dogs and cats, that we should take our battle directly to the streets. We might well have been junior OAS bringing the fight from Algeria to the streets of Paris. We were moving from the hills into an urban warfare scenario. I have no idea who thought of the idea, but I blame my older brother because someone had to be guilty, and it might just as well have been him. With pockets filled with *bombes,* we slipped out of our apartment, descended to the garage, then marched, single file, over rugged terrain without a GPS or satellite phone until we arrived at the top of the garage driveway and the corner of the street. We immediately threw several *bombes* at cars, some landing in front, some landing in back and some landing successfully and directly on cars. It was great sport until a car stopped midway up the street. We watched frozen as it backed up toward us on our one-way street. By that time, the three of us had dashed down the ramp, each of us choosing a car to hide under. I chose the family Peugeot, hoping somehow for divine protection, perhaps even intervention. We settled in our hiding places just as the driver of the mysterious car came down into the garage, yelling and cursing and calling us a litany of endearing names, such as *bande de voyous, petit crétins, imbéciles.* (Translated, it would be the equivalent of "such charming and well-behaved children." Sort of, or maybe "bunch of hooligans, brainless idiots." I prefer the well-behaved version.) It was like a bad movie. I saw his feet and heard his voice. Then the feet walked the entire length of the garage, each step echoing, then back again, then silence (old trick) while the feet waited for one of us to emerge from our hiding place.

I can only imagine what would have happened had the feet looked in my hiding place under the family car. He would have undoubtedly dragged me out by my feet, or my ears, and I would have been hauled off to the *gendarmerie* on the *Avenue du Roule,* where our Belgian nanny always warned I would end up. A *dossier* would have been started in my very own name. I would be fingerprinted, photographed and my *bombes* put away as state's evidence. I would have been taken to a dank, windowless interrogation room with a single light bulb, where two men in stained white shirts with sleeves rolled up, cigarettes glued to their lips and the pervasive smell of garlic sausage hovering over my face, would take turns questioning me closely. I would be shown pictures of suspects, some looking like little toughs, others as if they were about to cry. I would be pressed for information. To whom did I report? How did I communicate with other operatives? Who recruited me, and how was I recruited? Did I have any Algerian friends in Paris? Had I ever travelled to Algeria. And on and on, trying to sweat out a confession. Finally, I would have given in and demanded my dinner before giving up my brothers in arms.

It was getting late and there was school the next day. I would eventually be released and never allowed to do anything fun ever again in my life, that is, until the next hair-brained scheme came along.

Many years later, I made discrete inquiries, and yes, my dossier still existed, and it was considered "active."

An American Trilogy: Part 3 of 3

Before I was shuttled off to the *École Pascal,* the private school at 32-33 *Boulevard Lanne* in the 16th arrondissement, where I would be joining my two older brothers, I was marched up the *Avenue du Roule,* one of the two principal avenues in Neuilly, which led directly to the heart of Paris. My father led the way with my brothers trailing behind, trying vainly to kick my school bag out of my hands without being noticed. We were on our way to a small private school called the *Cours Montaigne.* The name sounded pleasant enough, conjuring up all sorts of fun learning events with the help of a nice teacher, who perhaps had just brought in the French equivalent of brownies to welcome the new student. Reality set in quickly. A tall, dark green fence covered in ivy faced the *Avenue du Roule* and stretched on until one reached the gated doorway with an elaborate wrought iron handle.

Once inside the grounds, you could see *la grande maison,* which looked like a junior mansion, and thinking back, I surmised it must have been a *hotel particulier.* F. Scott Fitzgerald would have found it to his liking, perhaps while he cooled his literary heels, waiting for Zelda to recover from alcoholism or a bout of depression at the American Hospital in Neuilly, just up the road. However, there was no lawn croquet in process, nor was anyone in bowler hats and striped jackets, nor elegant ladies in summer dresses and little parasols. The grounds were quiet with not a student to be seen anywhere, and I realized why. We were typically late, and this time we were late for my first day at school. The only thing that I could hear came from a simple, two-story residence turned school, where a class was now conjugating in three-part harmony. They might have also been waiving their little red books for all I knew.

Coming back to the *grande maison,* it was quite elegant with its sweeping marble stairs, leading to a handsome set of double doors with shiny brass in mass quantity. All very *comme il-faut,* and one got the impression it screamed, "Look, but don't dare touch anything, and that means you!" In front of *la grande maison,* there was a large and immaculately trimmed circular garden, bordered with flowers and a gravel walkway. The second building where I had heard the humming of well-behaved children with the fear of a higher power instilled in them, had four classrooms all equipped, as I remember, with the latest in radiator heating technology, circa the turn of someone's forgotten century. By then my family who had shepherded me had disappeared, leaving me to work the problem. I was shown to my class, located on the first floor, which I thought would allow me an easy escape. Our classroom was typical of the times with well-worn wooden desks and benches. I remember my bench had a fair amount of scratch marks, as well as a cleverly carved-out escape route. All desks were fitted with *encriers* or inkwells. The honor of filling the inkwells was reserved only for the well-behaved, top of the class, exemplary students or what we might know today as your classic kiss-ass. For some strange reason, I was never given the opportunity to pour ink and thankfully so because I am fairly sure I would have accidentally spilled it on someone. I would have been in jail for life. Accidents just happen to some people.

One day in class, I found myself doodling, absent-mindedly, instead of memorizing my verbs or studying for the inevitable *dictée*. The *dictée* was invented by a well-known French nobleman with a penchant for sadistic pleasures, I will let the reader guess who. The teacher would read one or two paragraphs, and the eager students would write it all down without any mistakes in spelling or punctuation with each letter perfectly shaped. I believe, to the best of my knowledge and recollection, that while trying to study, I found my mind drifting and writing descriptive and rather charming sentences about my teacher. Others would later say my notes were nothing short of disgusting and crude with all the evidence of someone badly brought up, much like a little American hoodlum. I miscalculated my desk partner's stupidity and his desire for self-preservation when I passed him my little verse for his eyes only. He laughed out loud, drawing unwanted attention from *Mademoiselle l'Institutrice*. I was clearly in a jam, and since I had no satellite phone, I could not call in an air strike to take care of the school, nor were there any drones over Neuilly ready for a surgical strike.

Mademoiselle demanded to see what my desk mate was now trying so desperately to hide. Within moment he caved like the spinless creature I knew he was, and the snitch handed over my work. Had I written it in English, I might have had a chance to bluff my way out of it, but no, it was all written down in French in excellent penmanship *sans fautes d'orthographe*, a factoid that was never mentioned at my trial. The snitch was immensely enjoying my predicament. I learned many years later that he had been run over by the number 43 bus on the *Avenue du Roule*. Urban justice or karma, what else can I say? In any event, prim and proper little *Mademoiselle*, fresh from passing her teacher's exams, was not about to let a simple infraction pass her by and escorted me out of the school building. We marched our way up the gravel walkway in silence until finally we reached the *grande maison*. For some reason, the house did not seem as inviting, and inside it smelled of *eau de javel*, that janitor in a drum and floor polish smell. The front doors closed behind us with a precision not seen since the days of *Monsieur Guillotin*.

I slowly followed *Mademoiselle* up the carpeted stairs and into a study. The only noise was the tick-tock from a gold mantle clock and the scratching sounds of an ink quill pen on paper. There behind the desk was the *grande dame* herself, *Madame la Directrice*, sitting with a shawl around her shoulders, silver hair wrapped in a bun so tightly her eyes seemed to bulge like some sort of science fiction creature. Finally, after what seemed like hours, she looked up and with a dismissive gesture pointed me to a chair. It seemed I was not going to be part of this little conversation, as a condemned man rarely is, I suppose. I listened as state's evidence was produced and reviewed before the judge, jury, and executioner, which was then followed by a look in my direction, not a look of "what a creative genius, he must be an American, we are so lucky to him in our school," but instead a look of disgust combined with complete and utter disappointment. I had failed the school, I had failed the French school system, and perhaps more importantly, I had failed France. I must say I knew all about "that look." It's one, I believe, that has been developed over time by French instructors over generations, and it's meant to be character-building for the student's benefit and ultimately for the glory of France. I would again see that look of disappointment when I joined my brothers at their school, when the *directeur* would hand me, or rather ship to me, my report card via air mail. The classroom enjoyed the moment, as I would dutifully go and retrieve it off the floor and thank the headmaster on high. But that is another story.

My sentence was handed down. At first, I expected to be put on a horse-drawn cart and taken for a severe haircut, but I was spared. For the next two weeks, I would be passing my recess in quiet, contemplative solitude by walking the courtyard. No one was to approach me, nor was I to talk to anyone. Oh, yes, I would be watched. So, for the next many recesses, I walked the perimeter alone, much to the amusement of my classmates, who found it necessary to taunt me in all sorts of ways. I remained in quiet contemplation, but not about my behavior. I was in fact quietly developing a battle plan of attack to storm la *grande maison,* capture *Madame la Directrice* and convict her of high crimes and misdemeanors.

Many years later, I returned to Neuilly-sur-Seine and wanted to visit the old stalag. I walked along Avenue du Roule but could not find what I remembered from so many years ago: the high green, ivied wall, the gate leading into the property, the *grande maison*, the school. Everything seemed to have vanished, and it was disconcerting. I had to find out what had happened, so naturally, I marched over to the *Mairie de Neuilly* (city hall), walked past the imperial guard with his machine gun, and presented my problem to the receptionist, who duly pointed me to the left, second room on the right, *Monsieur*. There, after crossing several hundred yards of highly polished parquet floors I was greeted by an attractive lady, sitting behind one of the world's largest, most ornate desks I have ever seen. She listened politely and patiently as I told her my story. Then she moved to her floor-to-ceiling bookcases. Reaching up to a shelf, she pulled down a dusty, overstuffed bound dossier. At her desk, she thumbed through several pages, then several more, and then looked at me over her glasses.

"Monsieur, I am sorry. There does not seem to be any record of a school by that name ever having been in Neuilly. Are you sure you are not possibly mistaken, perhaps in Paris?"

I assured Madame I was perfectly sane, even if I was an American. I did my best to be helpful with little factoids like small school, *Avenue du Roule, grande maison*, grey-haired witch, courtyard, Neuilly, dead snitch, and more.

The answer was still the same: "Monsieur, if the school is not listed in this dossier, then the school never existed. It is as simple as that. I am sorry I cannot be of further assistance."

The state is always right, even when it is wrong. For a moment, I wondered if I should have asked to see the original copy of my *certificat de naissance* (birth certificate), curious as to where it might be located and in which dossier. I wondered if it included any notations of my infractions against the state and my having been a bad *citoyen* and throwing firecrackers at little old ladies on the rue Perronet. Or perhaps my *certificat* was nicely framed or maybe hermetically sealed in a case for public viewing by little children as a warning. That seemed more likely to be the case. I got up, bid my farewell, and gingerly shook the thin, little hand that was offered to me. Not ready to be eaten, needs to be fattened up, I thought to myself.

I walked away more than a little frustrated and beginning to think that maybe I had been hallucinating all these years, which would have explained a lot. I walked back on the *Avenue du Roule* toward my metro stop when I passed a construction site, and something made me stop and look more closely. There tucked away in the back was indeed la *grande maison*! I knew it immediately, even after all these many years. It was slightly smaller than I remembered and certainly more weathered. It was undergoing much-needed renovations. The school building that had been on the left had completely vanished, bulldozed some years ago. Looking at the house brought back its share of memories, as you can imagine. I was transported back in time, once again a little boy, defiant against the French system and suffering the consequences. I stood there for a few moments longer, then turned away and slowly resumed my journey, feeling the chill of a late September afternoon.

I later learned a little more from researching *Le Figaro* newspaper, circa 1936.

LE COURS MONTAIGNE A NEUILLY 58, avenue du Roule, à Neuilly-sur Seine, *près de la porte Maillot et du Bois de Boulogne, on aperçoit un immeuble de proportions élégantes au milieu d'un vaste jardin c'est le Cours Montaigne. Le Cours Montaigne est une institution si bien tenue que, vieux seulement de cinq ans, il compte déjà 215 élèves, externes et demi-petit pensionnaires.*

Clearly, I needed to send this to the kind folks at the *mairie*, who insisted that no such school ever existed. Ram that little bit of reality down their throat. Perhaps, I did learn something after all from *Cours Montaigne*.

ALUMNI DAZE OR MY PERSONAL *RENTRÉE SCOLAIRE* (THE START OF THE SCHOOL YEAR)

*A*fter leaving one school in Neuilly-sur-Seine, I found myself joining my two older brothers at the École Pascale in the 16e. I like to think that the first school realized that my brain power and intellectual capacity were just too much to manage. Honestly, I don't recall whether I was invited to leave the little school in Neuilly, or if my father made a sober assessment that three unruly Americans were perhaps easier to handle under one school roof. That may have proved to have been a slight miscalculation on someone's part. Just saying.

Many years later, I returned to France and Paris, having decided that it was time to face my demons, real or imagined. I recalled vividly that I could not wait to leave that school and most certainly swore that would never return on my own free will. Time changes things.

The old school before the new one was built in the 1950s.

In the interest of health, I decided to take a long stroll to the school, walking from the *Champs-Elysées* down to the Avenue Foch, the widest street in Paris and where, it seemed, every possible motorbike dealership was located. From there, I walked to the *Port Dauphine* and hung a left onto a long broad stretch of road bordering the *Bois de Boulogne* and known informally as the *Boulevards des Maréchaux,* so named because sections of the grand boulevard are named after famous Napoleonic *maréchals* like *Lannes* and *Suchet*. We were now in the 16e *arrondissement* of Paris, an area made up of rather chic and exclusive residential districts like *Auteuil* (where my father had lived as a boy) and *Passy,* all with large *Haussmanian*-style grand apartments gracefully bordering the *Bois de Boulogne*. This area includes many diplomatic embassies, as well as museums, including the *Musée Marmottan,* which holds some of Monet's best works, and sporting arenas.

My destination was the *École Pascal,* an excellent private school founded in 1899. Now some 120 years later, it is still thriving and doing well with an enrollment of 100 students. The school was originally located 27-29 *Boulevard Lannes,* but now the new school sits close to the old one at 33 *Boulevard Lannes.* It was then and still is now both a boarding (*interne*) and day (*externe*) school. The school hosted many students whose parents were ambassadors, dignitaries, or leaders from various French-speaking countries.

Standing outside, I must confess that I had some real trepidations about going back in for a host of reasons. Not being the sharpest tool in the shed (something that I admitted after repeated slaps), I was intellectually challenged in my French studies, which left me with a bullseye on my back. I was one of three Americans, the other two being my two older brothers. My father, years back, had the pleasure of being a student at the school back in the early 1930s for just a short while before being sent to boarding school in Switzerland for boys whose parents were drowning in money, like the young Shah of Iran, as an example. I recall that my oldest brother's teacher clearly remembered my father while he had been a student at Pascal. Hard to run away from that painful legacy. Clearly what was good for my father had to be good for all us. Therein lay my father's logic.

We would normally start our school day behind the eight ball, as we were habitually late, only to find the school's front doors locked for the duration of the morning assembly. No sneaking-in, which meant one had to bang on the glass doors and yell until the assistant headmaster with his severe grey crew cut and pencil-thin mustache showed up, visibly perturbed, and reluctantly let us in, but only after a moment of reflection. That particular morning drill got really old really fast, and we could never seem to get my father into the car any faster than he wanted to. We always had to make a quick stop at the *cafe-bar-tabac* on the *Avenue du Roule* to pick up a pack of Royals cigarettes. After assembly, we made our way to our various classrooms with the help of obliging hall monitors, *pions* as they were called (i.e., *personne qui surveille l'étude dans un établissement scholaire*). In other words, junior goons, whose job it was to herd everyone to class, and so they often employed various unorthodox means to accomplish the job. From the administration's point of view, the goons helped facilitate a smooth and orderly scholastic day.

My class day was usually spent trying to avoid the teacher by unsuccessfully hiding behind a larger head. It never worked. The teacher, *l'institutrice,* bless her heart, had ice in her veins. You could feel the love. Repeated efforts with her hand in a forward motion and in the general direction of my face served as a reminder of my personal failings. It never seemed to produce the desired effect of my wanting to become a model French *citoyen*. I will not go into more details, but by the end of the day, running away and living in the *Bois de Boulogne* seemed, at the time, like a pretty darn good idea. One story I relate to my grandchildren was the day someone in authority decided that they needed to show other classes just what a bad student looked like. Even better if he is an American. Extra points. Off we went, me slightly on tiptoes and one ear firmly in the hand of the school assistant principal. After showing me off to several classes as an example of what bad students looked like, he got tired of the game, and I was returned to my classroom, one ear noticeably red. In recounting this story to my grandchildren, they would look at me as if I were from another planet, especially when I would point to one ear declaring that they could see for themselves that my one ear was forever lower than the other. Forever, I tell you!

A little side bar: Speaking of the *Bois de Boulogne*, I remember one time we had a field trip to the *Bois* as part of our "let's draw nature" class. There was a sudden commotion, and a sense of excitement rippled through the students, who then started running in the direction of a little lady in a raincoat. Students were circling around her like a pack of hounds with pen in hand. I asked one of my classmates what was all the fuss about, and he answered,

"Why, that's Édith Piaf!" I replied, "So, who's that?"

The person who most epitomized the school, at least in my mind, was the headmaster. Put away those thoughts of Goodbye Mr. Chips, a kindly, old gentlemen as it were, with a pocket watch in his waistcoat, perhaps with a wisp of white hair and a twinkle in his eye. No, this gentleman was the very definition of authoritarianism. At the end of the school day, he would stand at the top of the steps just outside his office and within easy reach of any student who foolishly decided that now was a good time to misbehave. The older portion of the school building still had a potato cave and a small, barred window at pavement level. It was no longer used for storing potatoes, obviously, but every so often it became the temporary home for certain students. Although I personally never saw it, my older brother once told me that he arrived at school one morning and saw a hapless boy peering out through the barred window. Could have been just an urban legend, of course. An interesting historical tidbit in all of these musings is that, apparently, when the headmaster was a young teacher, he would stand out on his class balcony. In June 1940, he watched as an endless parade of German soldiers, tanks and guns followed by more soldiers and tanks until he finally realized he was watching the same parade over and over again. The German army, in an effort to demonstrate a show of overwhelming force, were looping the parade through Paris over and over again. Much like a bad movie rerun on television.

Making my way inside the school the headmaster personally welcomed me back. To legitimize my status, I dropped a few teachers' names, as well as one of his predecessor's name. That did it. In a blink of an eye, I had broken the code, whereupon the headmaster latched on to one student, Dominique, telling me he was one of our brightest boys and would personally give me a guided tour of the school. Everything, kitchen, dorms, and all. The school was my oyster. The conquering hero had returned. Long live me! After you have seen one classroom, that was about it. One thing I do recall was a class of boys and girls who were around my same age when I was there. My trusty guide briefed the teacher who then announced to the class, "Pay attention everyone! Here is a former student and visiting from, no less, the United States!" One boy started whispering to his classmate, whereupon the teacher turned to the unfortunate lad and said, since he obviously had something important to say, we should all hear it. The poor boy was promptly directed to stand in front of this distinguished visitor and share. I felt that long-forgotten knot, twisting deep down in my stomach. The slow acid drip returned. It was all I could do to stop myself from saying, "Run, little boy, run as fast as you can. I'll cover for you."

A French Butcher May be the Nearest Thing to God

What could be more holy than a French butcher shop? Before you laugh, I am dead serious. In France, most people are quite familiar with their butcher, and it's usually the *boucher du quartier*, the neighborhood butcher. If you don't know a good butcher, you do your best to seek out your friends and pry out the name of one. One's relationship with one's butcher is serious business. It's very personal, like religion, just a tad tastier.

I stopped in to see Marcel (not his real name of course, because that is privileged information). I address him as *Monsieur le Boucher* because I still have some residue of good manners. Truly, he is a butcher par excellence. He always has his white butcher's coat on, which always appears miraculously spotless. I am waiting for the day when I will see him in a meat-stained *tablier,* waving his cleaver in his hand and someone's head in the other. Marcel is usually behind the counter, helping customers, who carefully listen to his recommendations on a cut of meat that's worth buying that day. I am always amazed at his multitasking skills. He can be working the string around a plump *gigot* of some sort, slapping meat down on the scale, maneuvering his meat cleaver through a loin chop, or wrapping up a customer's package with such tender loving care, as if it were a present for his little girl, Julie. But always a smile (for the most part) and a little chat about something important like the weather or commiserating about the absence of a cut of meat, or sadly admitting he has sold the last of his broiled chickens and potatoes. Those chickens always go fast, and no wonder. They are in plain view outside, as they turn on skewers all day, browning and cooking ever so slowly, their juices dripping and collecting into the receiving arms of the baby potatoes below.

In Defense of Good Manners:
La Politesse Avant Tout

I came across a menu written on a chalkboard and was immediately drawn to it. I understood what was clearly being stated, but not spoken. In English-speak, rude people are more than welcomed; however, they should expect to pay a premium for their rudeness. I like that very much. Or customers could reach deep down and find some semblance of civility. The rude-risk premium would then be adjusted accordingly. Finally, if a

191

customer knows better and had been slapped around enough in their younger years for being rude, then politeness was hardly an afterthought. There would be no rude-risk premium at all. Life is sweet. Do we Americans generally turn rude once we step off that plane into a foreign country? I wonder if it's perhaps a defense mechanism. The thinking could go something like this: I cannot speak your language, dude, and you can't speak mine, which makes you really stupid, and I don't do stupid. Therefore, I can be rude. I overgeneralize to be sure, but just a little, I suspect. Politeness in French society is akin to godliness. Maybe more so. Let's just say that I happen to know from experience that the French system expects, no demands is more like it, that to be a model citizen, to be successful in French society and to rise above the flotsam and jetsam, by default the lower classes, politeness is a prerequisite. Nothing is more telling than bad manners. I think my parents told me that on more than one occasion!

Another glass of wine Monsieur? Why yes, don't mind if I do. And thank you!

We Have Examined Your Dossier, Monsieur

*J*ust recently, I was having a conversation with some colleagues on the subject of *le dossier*. Nothing is done, nothing can be done, and nothing will be done without a *dossier*. It is, I suppose, comforting to have the masses so regimentally structured. Folks in the USA tend to have high anxiety over our bureaucracy, but I tell them they should all relax and experience real anxiety abroad. A dossier in its simplest form is just a collection of papers containing detailed information about a person or subject (usually a person's police, credit, marriage, and divorce records.) A dossier can mean a folder, a file, and it can even refer to where you place your back against a chair. There are big, bulging dossiers, like the U.N. dossier or the Warren Commission dossier. There are many dossiers that never existed, and police investigation dossiers. There are disarmingly nice little dossiers like the *dossier de marriage* with little cupids on it. Inside is an exhaustive list of documents to produce, which must be stamped, signed, attested, or otherwise notarized. The very word *dossier* evokes a sense of dread, no doom perhaps is better. At least for me, it does. I do not really know why, but I tend to conjure up images of myself enjoying a quiet Paris afternoon in the fall at a bistro somewhere, nursing an *apero*, when all of a sudden, I am lifted out of my chair and dragged to the curb just as a black Citroen comes screeching to a halt. Two burly, helpful attendants in raincoats and badly in need of a shower proceed to stuff my 6-foot frame in the back seat, then stuff themselves on either side of me.

I must admit that feel a bit like the ham and cheese in a Croque Monsieur. No one's talking. Your mind races, as it always does in these types of situations, thinking about all the things you could have done wrong. Did you walk out without paying a bill? Did the smiling young lady at the *boulangerie* really think you looked like a wanted type, he must surely be from Marseilles? Is your passport still valid? Are you a day over your visa *sejour*? Did someone, somewhere mistakenly finger you as some underworld drug lord, even a spy? What a laugh! Nothing is funny when you're finally dragged into the prefecture (a mere formality, of course) and then placed in front of an oh-so-busy civil servant, looking bored, but taking all the time in the world to finish a task of vital importance to the *République,* or maybe it's the football pool. On his desk, you see, is an overstuffed, leather-bound, accordion-style dossier, bearing your last name in capital letters, followed by your first initial. So, you sit there, taking in the cloud of blue cigarette smoke, as you begin to feel the first unmistakable drip-drip of sweat running down your back. Maybe an old ceiling fan is turning ever so slowly, and each time with a little squeak that only grows more pronounced until it resembles a blood-curling scream inside your head! Of course, this would all be shot in black and white.

Let me discuss a hypothetical case of someone who has been in Paris for a few months and decides that they want to rent a larger apartment. Walking in with your ballpoint pen, ready to fill out an application, is not going to cut the *moutarde*, unless you just happen to have your dossier tucked under your arm with copies of three months of pay slips and proof of employment, so as to be sure you are not on any *plan social* or welfare. You need proof of insurance that covers your rent for 36 months, should you decide to stop paying and skip out, as well as your RIB, which means *relève indentité bancaire*, which is worth its weight in gold and means you have a French bank account. Without a bank account, you have no real status, and without any status you are unrecognizable as a person by the state. You also need a statement from your existing landlord that says you reside in their building, a copy of your landlord's ID card, a copy of your landlord's gas bill, and a copy of your passport.

I almost forgot to mention that it is entirely possible that your dossier will need a document certifying that you cannot produce any tax documents, if you have not been in France long enough, and a document saying that you have dutifully handed in your tax declaration for the current year. It's only a couple of things that you can quickly put your hands on.

Are you sure that is all? Incredibly good question because if you do not know the right questions to ask, then a most polite administrative official won't tell you. If you appreciate Kafka, then you will feel right at home. You cannot know, and you won't know what you really need to know until its review time. It is that lovely little process where the dossier is examined to ascertain if it conforms to all rules and regulations, likely promulgated under the Napoleonic code. No exceptions, Monsieur! Sometimes, even when you have done your homework and checked, no double checked, to make sure everything is in the dossier, when it gets reviewed, you must accept the fact that something will be missing, not for reasons of having completely messed up, but for reasons of administration. If you are experiencing an administrative difficulty, you may well be asked, encouraged, to resubmit your request in writing. The state lets you know ahead of time that their answer will be "No." You are, however, urged to make the request to the state anyway. That, too, by the way, will go in your dossier.

One day, Monsieur, when your dossier is of no further interest to us, it will be filed away for reference purposes only. If the information contained inside or your identity is too sensitive, your dossier will be destroyed, along with all records of it ever having existed. That is all I am at liberty to say. We will of course have to start a new dossier on you. Thank you for coming down to the *prefecture de police. Bonne journée, Monsieur.* But in the vie *quotidienne* of most French men and women, the dossier is simply an indispensable bureaucratic necessity in order to do or get just about anything. If it's not *"un dossier"* then it's an *"affaire."* I'm not sure which one is worse.

Yours truly has a dossier or two, as well. True enough. A dossier with my birth certificate, signed and officially stamped and sealed with my father's attestation, and all residing somewhere deep within the bowels of the *mairie de Neuilly-sur-Seine*. It is alive and well because I had to obtain a copy for a wild goose chase. Enter the *dossier de marriage*, which is stored somewhere in a *mairie* in eastern France. But that is a story for another book. It was all a moment of weakness, a moment of wild abandonment. The dossier will surely note that madame's information was completed to perfection like a good student, but monsieur's information was started, but because of incomplete information or lack of interest or a moment of lucidity or maybe just history of being a bad student, was terminated. I would be a fool to believe they would summarily trash my file or burn it for a weenie roast. In one of my many past lives, I was a bureaucrat, and the state does not do such foolish things.

Ms. Edith's Travel Agency: French Dreams for Sale

"Paris is a place in which we can forget ourselves, reinvent, expunge the dead weight of our past."
Michael Simkins, "Detour de France: An Englishman in Search of a Continental Education"

Ms. Edith St. Germain matter-of-factly pushed down a single window blind with a well-polished fingernail, for just long enough to see the snowflakes beginning to fall ever so gently like little white parachutes, one after the other, and landing perfectly onto the quiet street below. She watched for a moment longer, as the pavement seemed to almost magically pull up its fluffy white blanket and disappear underneath. They had called for snow, at least that's what Ms. Edith remembered from reading the *Daily Courier,* but only after first consulting her horoscope, which oddly enough had made no mention of inclement weather. She liked reading her horoscope almost as much as she enjoyed reading about the weather, as both gave her sense of purpose and direction for the day ahead. Besides, it was something she could look forward to. The streetlights were coming on now, a flicker of light here, and then finally their full light cast a wintery glow onto the street and beyond.

It was an early evening in December, and the hustle and bustle of the rush hour had long since died down, leaving but a few weary stragglers walking by without so much as a glance at Ms. Edith's storefront. Couples arm-in-arm with their holiday bundles and a young man she recognized from the next building had decided to take his dog for an early and hopeful evening walk. The occasional businessman, clutching his briefcase, head down against the wind, hurryingly marching forward, determined not to miss the last commuter train that would afford him safe passage from the city and out to the comfort and safety of his suburbia.

There had been no customer inquiries at the travel agency that day. In fact, there had been no customers at all that week, perhaps with the exception of the mailman, who brought the usual assortment of bills, some with late notices and endless holiday advertisements. Everyone was wrapped up in the frenzy of the Christmas season and distressingly far from anyone's minds were thoughts about glamorous destinations around the world, and sadly, Ms. Edith's superior and unparalleled travel services. Yes, maybe that was forgotten for now, but she was resolute about one thing: All of that would change. "*Bien sûr*, how could it not?" After a dreary winter, spring would make itself known, and with that, surely there would be dreams of Paris in the springtime. Where else would reasonable people want to go? Ms. Edith thought that a cruise on the Danube or perhaps even a visit to Florence, which could certainly be lovely in the spring, were fine destinations indeed, but they would never measure up to her passion for Paris, the City of Light. Yes, they would come. Ms. Edith stubbornly clung to that belief. They would come if for no other reason than to be in Paris in the springtime. It was just that simple.

The Travel Dreams Agency, owned and operated by one Ms. Edith St. Germain, formerly known as Ms. Edith Wyzgowski before adopting St. Germain as her *nom de plume* in honor of the Boulevard St. Germain in the 6e arrondissement. The travel agency was located on the north end of Wabash Avenue, one block from the intersection of Wabash and Belvedere and close to the elevated L, which rattled past with regularity from early morning well into the night. A passersby could hardly miss the large travel posters scotch taped to her front window, posters urging you to visit one exciting part of the world after another. Crowding out frayed posters of Athens, Rome or Bora Bora was an oversized poster of a smiling Pan Am stewardess, beckoning you to come aboard the clipper jet service with direct flights from New York's La Guardia to Paris Orly Airport.

When it came to travel planning generally, and Paris in particular, Miss Edith knew her stuff, alright. Some even said she was hands-down better than any other travel agent in town! That was in her heyday, they added with just a trace of a smile. Listening to Miss Edith go on as she did with only the mere gentle of encouragement, you would think she and Edith Piaf, the iconic French songstress, had at one time strolled, arm-in-arm, down the majestic avenues in Paris with such famous actors as John Paul Belmondo or perhaps even Carry Grant likely trailing not far behind. Of course, there would always be photojournalists following their every step. No autographs, please! The crowds grew in size with each story, or at least so it seemed. It was carefully orchestrated to enchant young lovers, newlyweds, and couples alike who were contemplating a travel to the continent and many for the first time. The stories were magical, and everyone wanted to believe each and every last one of them. Miss Edith represented Paris. She had lived there and knew her way around the alleys and boulevards of Paris. But truth is often what you want it to be, and if truth be known, it was Edith's mother who had been in Paris so many years ago. At that time, she was named after her mother's best friend, Edith Piaf. A little white lie here and there could be forgiven because, after all, Paris was a city for lovers, and all things were excused on that basis alone, including a little embellishment when necessary to seal a round-trip package to the City of Light. Money was, after all, money in any currency.

As long as she could remember, Miss Edith had grown up with her mother's stories about Paris and places with such mysterious names as Clichy, Chaillot, Montmartre, *le Left Bank, Boulevard St. Germain*, le Moulin Rouge and the Crazy Horse Saloon. It was intoxicating to Miss Edith. She lived for her mother's stories as much as her mother loved reliving them, maybe more. Together they had watched almost every movie they could lay their hands set in Paris in some fashion, from "An American in Paris" to "The Last Tango in Paris" and everything else in between. Both mother and daughter became part of the movies. They were there in Paris, singing and dancing in cabarets, drinking champagne, at the races in Longchamp, round and around the Arc de Triomphe and to the Eiffel Tower and back, and being wooed by the finest of movie stars. Ms. Edith had long ago memorized the lines of her favorite actresses on the silver screen and would amuse her clientele as much as she had delighted her mother with nonchalant shrugs of her shoulders, holding a cigarette from her brightly red painted lips and singing a few notes from Edith Piaf's "*Non, Je ne regrette rien.*" Fact and fiction were artfully blurred into a well-rehearsed exotic mixture, a dream tailored to each of her clients. Ms. Edith lived vicariously through each and every one them. When reality chose not to intrude, she expected at any moment to see Charles Boyer, Jean Gabin or perhaps Jean Kelly burst through the front door, each declaring their everlasting love and saying, "Please, Mademoiselle Edith, come wiz me to Paree." She clung stubbornly to that dream and the anticipation of one day being swooped away by her knight in shining armor, who most likely wore a beret.

The snow had not let up all evening. The street was now even quieter and deserted than before. Ms. Edith opened a window and felt the rush of icy air hitting her face. Quickly closing the window and latching it shut, she then turned on her record player and sat in a comfortable armchair and listened as her namesake slowly led her away to another place and time. She was happy and content now.

Allez, venez, Milord
Vous asseoir à ma table
Il fait si froid, dehors
Ici c'est confortable
Laissez-vous faire, Milord
Et prenez bien vos aises
Vos peines sur mon cœur
Et vos pieds sur une chaise
Je vous connais, Milord
Vous n'm'avez jamais vue

Je ne suis qu'une fille du port
Qu'une ombre de la rue...

Edith Piaf '59
(& merci à George Moustaki)

THE HOUSE AT TWELVE GINGER LANE: FROM BEIJING TO PARIS: FROM CHOPSTICKS TO CROISSANTS

Beijing: Dazed and Confused

I was directed, or should I say wordlessly pointed, in the general direction of a massive public square. "Down this road?" I asked again, raising my voice so as to be better understood. The old man nodded and smiled a toothless smile, then again pointed as if he already knew my destination.

I walked down the well-worn, winding, narrow street once known as Ginger Lane and now little more than an odd historical curiosity, a side road that somehow had managed to fend off the demolition derby of the people's relentless march toward progress in this, the City of Heavenly Tranquility. Was I hoping to find by chance some overlooked bit of memorabilia, forgotten from the days of the Legation Quarter with its history of diplomacy and intrigue, missions jostling for power and advantage, scandals, grand dining, and white mischief from days gone by? Perhaps I might even find that quaint, old-world restaurant, tucked away at No. 12. Surely, it still served a heady variety of exotic Asian-European dishes. With its ceiling fans straining mightily to move the still air, the charming hostess with a warm and inviting smile would beckon me to a corner table with a small delicate vase of flowers on a freshly starched tablecloth. As evening approached, I would watch from my table as the lantern lights along Ginger Lane would come aglow, one slowly after the other. From somewhere off in the distance, I heard the faint, scratchy sound of music straining from an old gramophone. A woman's laughter, clear at first then slowly drifting away.

Paris: Dazed and Hungry

Caté Bergamote is a cozy little restaurant nestled on the Left Bank at 8, *rue Montfaucon* in the 6th *arrondisement*, an area considered by many to represent the quintessential Parisian neighborhood. It's colorful, exciting, and maybe a little pricey. One does not casually stumble onto Bergamote. You have to know where you are going, or perhaps you are *du quartier* and thus (smugly) in the know.

I had just arrived that afternoon from Beijing and had made plans for a late dinner. From my little hotel, I made my way to the restaurant, working my way through an army of eager, impatient customers all waiting to be seated and told Madame that I had a reservation for 10 p.m. Madame was multitasking and waved me off, as if I was some pesky fly bothering her or perhaps someone trying to sell flowers or maybe one of those darling little Eiffel Tower trinkets. Look at the details, Monsieur, while some urchin makes off with your wallet. No more room, no reservations, we are full, *Monsieur*. Come back tomorrow, please and thank you. But I stubbornly insisted on my rights as an American in Paris (not exactly placing me on firm legal footing, I realized), letting her know in Parisian French that I had called ahead, out of consideration, just to be sure.

"*Aahh, c'est vous, Monsieur, qui nous a téléphoner ?*"

"*Et bien, oui, c'est moi,*" I replied, sounding just slightly perturbed and French enough. I was directed to wait over by the bar, an area squashed between the cash register with bread being sliced in a frenzy by a hurried waiter and a table with two customers hunched over salads and a bottle of wine. I felt as if I should introduce myself, if only I could have turned around. I was thirsty and wanted a tall glass of water but having been in China less than 24 hours ago, I was wary of any kind of water from anywhere. I made a command decision and ordered a supersized *pression 1664,* which arrived cold and disappeared with remarkable ease. I was ready for dinner, and it just so happened my table was ready for me. I love those kinds of coincidences. I followed the almond-eyed lady to my table.

I was seated by a window, better to view the hungry masses, and me without any cake to offer. Madame came by, or perhaps swooped by, making sure I was seated comfortably and had a menu. Progress was being made at last, I quickly ordered a *pichet* of *rouge* to get me in the zone. My body clock was on Chinese time. I was floating in some blurred time zone, but lucid enough to recognize what I needed was a good home-cooked French meal. I knew I would not be disappointed. The wine arrived, followed shortly by a basket of bread. I was famished and thirsty. In between long coifs from my *Côtes du Rhône,* I marveled over each piece the crusty bread. I perused the menu ever so slowly, refusing to skip over any dish. I was squeezing out every ounce of enjoyment and loving every minute. I finally gave in and decided

I would start with the *terrine de foie gras de canard maison,* or as we know it, home-made duck foie gras, flavored with vanilla and tarragon. When have we not made that before? More bread, and yes, my wine was looking a little low in the glass. If heaven could have a taste, I was there. I wanted to stand up, pump my fist in the air and yell "Oh, yeah, now were talking, oh, yeah!" But instead, I just settled in more comfortably. My culinary three-act play was just starting. I gripped the menu firmly with both hands, surveying my choices. Maybe a skirt steak with shallots and fine herbs or perhaps red mullet fillets with coarsely chopped tomatoes and basil or maybe...

Heady moments indeed and then, in a single moment, I decided on the *magret de canard, sauce au miel et romarin* or duck breast with honey and rosemary sauce. "Excellent choice, Monsieur, very popular this evening." Isn't that always the case, I wondered to myself. I poured myself just a little more red wine and amusingly pondered the rather stark culinary differences found in the two capital cities: Paris and Beijing. My order arrived, or shall I say presented, with a flourish, and *voilà,* Monsieur. More bread appeared. My glass was refilled, and I had my fork and knife at the ready. Do not mess with me on the question of French food, *s'il vous plaît!* It looked fabulous and tasted more than delicious. It was tender and tasty and delicately and perfectly put together. I just love the magic in good cooking. Was I interested in seeing the dessert list? Seriously? I caved, as I was beyond putting up any resistance, real or imagined. I concluded my extravaganza, my reentry into culinary sanity, with a *gratin de bananes et sa glace coco* or oven-grilled bananas with coconut ice cream. The little *serveuse* smiled and purred,

"Did you know that's my favorite dessert, too!" Will wonders never cease, I thought to myself.

Moments later, American Express was handling the bill, and soon I was tucked away in my ever-so-comfy bed, the mattress swallowing me up, and I dreamed of Pecking ducks in red hats, marching along the *Boulevard St. Germain* and masquerading as *magret de canard.*

Falling In Love in Clichy

I suppose you could say it all started that rainy night in Clichy when I heard a melancholy tune being sung, and the voice beckoned me like a siren song, pulling in toward her all those who would listen. Let me explain. Some years ago, back in the days when I had no fixed address, I smoked cheap French unfiltered cigarettes, drank house wine like a fool, worked odd jobs and lived in an attic studio that was steamy in the summer and frigid all winter. I used to think that I could not have been any happier than I was then. Every week, I would drop by the American Express office to pick up what mail I had, perhaps a note from home, asking if I was still planning on returning and if I was finished with my foolish grand experiment. Sometimes, if I was lucky, there would be a certified check to help me make it through to the next month. I was usually living on fumes and indeed grateful for that check and would treat myself to a fine meal and a full *pichet* of wine at one of my several bistro hangouts.

There were times, quite often actually, when I would find myself exploring the wonders of the *Boulevard de Clichy* in the part of Paris fondly known as *Pigalle*. I suppose a healthy amount of curiosity drew me there initially because it was a favorite destination of tourists of all stripes, but more importantly, it offered a selection of amusements literally from A to Z. I remember my father telling me stories about Paris nights, and maybe that added to my youthful interest. *Pigalle* was customer service-oriented all the way and with a French twist to make it all the more memorable. So, with a Boy Scout's sense of mission and determination, I made a point of visiting every seedy little establishment in the quartier that professed to offer some sort of entertainment and garnered some memorable moments, while other moments I have chosen to quietly forget.

Over time, I found myself making frequent stops at a smoky club aptly called, given the neighborhood, *Aux Petits Anges* (the Little Angels). I was never quite sure where the concept of angels fit in, other than the two little angels on either side of the door. Perhaps there was some sort of existential meaning behind it all that I failed to grasp, until one Sunday evening in October. I had just dined at a corner bistro, having enjoyed a tasty bowl of fish stew, moped up with a baguette and washed down with a couple of glasses of coarse red *maison* or house wine, when I decided to walk toward Clichy. I remember it as if it were yesterday. It was chilly and damp with a light drizzle. Paris seemed dreary that night as I made my way toward the Little Angels when I heard a haunting voice singing a familiar Edith Piaf tune:

> *Tu me fais tourner la tête, mon manège à moi c'est toi. Je suis toujours à la fête, quand tu m'prends dans tes bras. Je ferais le tour du monde, Ça ne tourn'rait pas plus qu'ça. La terre n'est pas assez ronde, pour m'étourdir autant qu'toi...*

The voice was a dead ringer for the Little Sparrow. I peered through one of *Aux Petits Anges's* windows to have a quick look and satisfy my curiosity. I saw her there, sitting on a stool in front of the microphone. Stepping inside, through a haze of blue cigarette smoke, I saw Marilou, who was clearly dressed to impress the tourist crowd, who were indeed gawking at her while pretending they understood every word she sang. She wore a black, studded motorcycle jacket, striped jersey, a skirt that looked like she had been poured into, and a pair of dangerously high heels. Her beret slanted down and the ever-present *Gitane* cigarette glued to her red, full lips completed the picture. That night, I, too, was a tourist, my eyes fixated on Marilou, wishing the night would never end. In the ensuing weeks and months and into Christmas, Marilou and I saw each other after hours as often as we could, and I even managed to convince her not to return to Marseilles, but to stay and work in Paris. It was good for Clichy and the tourists. It was good for the owner of the Little Angels, but it was even better for me.

That Christmas, we spent hours walking arm in arm, looking in all the store windows on the Boulevard Haussmann, always stopping at a cafe, sitting under a standing heater with a hot drink whenever we were too cold to walk any further. Very quickly, it seemed, we had created our own *complicité,* that level of closeness and intimacy that builds between couples. We found a studio apartment on the fifth floor of a building in Montparnasse, equipped with all the comforts of home, no elevator, a *minuterie* on each floor, and an inquisitive, nosy concierge. Above our apartment, we had a family of five with continually crying children and the ever-present sound of one unfortunate or another being slapped into good behavior. Next to us lived a Russian émigré couple, who would often get noisy, usually after midnight, and hurl vodka-soaked Russian invectives at each other. On the other side of us was a wounded veteran from the French and Algerian war. He always was quiet and dignified. He seemed nice and once even brought us a bottle of Algerian wine and a plate of cakes. Shortly after that, we learned from Madame la Concierge that he had hung himself. "I'm not at all surprised," she said. "I saw it coming, he had too many demons to cope with," she whispered, "but at least he paid the rent!"

Despite all that, we discovered a little restaurant *du quartier, Chez Janot,* which is still there today, and we very quickly made it our place. Over time, we eventually became friends with the owners. But I suppose all good things must come to an end, even in Paris.

I came home one evening to find Marilou had left leaving a note that said simply, *"Au revoir, cheri. Je m'en vais et je retourne à Marseille,"* and in a nano second my world collapsed around me.

THANKSGIVING DINNER IN LIBERATED PARIS

There was undoubtedly much reason to give thanks that Thanksgiving Day in Paris, 1944. After all, the City of Light had been liberated by Allied forces with General De Gaulle's Free French army leading the way into the city, as a matter of honor and pure politics for the general and for the Allies, harmonious international relations. The German army was, relatively speaking, on the run, though ugly battles in Holland and Belgium surely lay ahead. But for now, an end to the war in Europe, which had scorched the continent, was a real and very distinct possibility. Spirits must surely have been high that day in November.

I have to wonder what was going through the minds of all those seated at that Thanksgiving dinner table at an undetermined location somewhere in Paris on Nov. 23, 1944. My father, dark hair receding, is seated at the table in the upper left of the photo, his head tilted back. He's staring expectantly at the camera, as if saying, "Make it quick." The exact location for this gathering of OSS members and most likely their counterparts from other Allied intelligence agencies is unknown at least to me. Perhaps I was too young to have known how to ask my father the right questions, which was, more often than not, the usual case growing up. Drawing out any information from my father relative to his OSS and specifically his X-2 days in CI during the war, be it London, Paris and elsewhere, was a futile effort, as it was, I suspect, with others whose fathers or mothers had been with the OSS and sworn to secrecy to their dying days. My father's professional life, which essentially was a continuation of his OSS days, until he finally retired and came in from the cold, ensured that little, if any, information was ever gleamed by yours truly. That is, other than the information he chose to selectively part within an answer (vague as it was) to my questions. If you did not know what questions to ask, then you were relegated to fumbling in the dark. Yours truly rarely saw the light of day.

As a curious foodie, I had to wonder, what were they having for dinner? Was it Mom's 21-pound turkey with stuffing, mashed potatoes, cranberry sauce, yams, giblet gravy and fluffy rolls? Oh, let's not forget those creamed onions and the trifecta the mince, pumpkin, and pecan pies! I think we all know the answer to that question. I have been to other Thanksgiving dinners given by expats here and there around the world, as we gathered together, just as those in the photo were gathered to celebrate being together with family and close friends to give thanks. The extensive planning, preparation and coordination required to have a successful Thanksgiving dinner is, I would argue, on the same level as planning for the D-Day invasion. Long-held family traditions and customs inevitably surface. (Why the lima beans? Because we do that every year, dear, that's why). Some humorous, some more awkward than anything else. Who will bring what? Please, can we not have the Jell-O salad again this year? Who is Uncle George bringing to dinner this time, and has anyone met her? Remember the one last year? She got drunk and started dancing with Dad. Oh, and Grandfather is bringing a secret, special dish, something he had in India, and now we all have to have at least a taste. After all, it's Thanksgiving. Who will say grace before dinner? Please make it short and leave out Pilgrim politics and the Indians and who did what to whom! What do you mean, the cable is not working? What about the football games you all watch while sleeping on the sofa? This meal, this tradition, is a unique American phenomenon and is celebrated in most, if not all, homes in America, just as it is among expats wherever they may gather, be it Marbella, Spain, Jakarta, Indonesia, Kinshasa, DRC or Johannesburg, South Africa. In fact, anywhere.

I have to say that it's a bit challenging to try and be a culinary detective, given the scant evidence presented in the photo. In all likelihood, I suspect no one ran out to shoot a turkey in Paris, and the meal consisted of what was actually available, although our troops may have brought one or two uniquely American items to contribute to the dinner, so as to make it feel a little more like home. The OSS men and women, I suspect, fared much better in terms of food than the average GI who was battling it out across France, but on the other hand, it was certainly not dinner at *Maxim's*, *Lapérouse*, *La Tour d'Argent*, or the Ritz. The black market was still very much alive, as it had been throughout the war, and prices certainly did not plummet after the Americans paraded down the Champs-Elysees! Good food was available if you had the right contacts. For example, there was a restaurant on the *Rue de Sèvres* that relied on family connections somewhere in Brittany for its meat supply and there was a butcher on the *Rue Marbeuf* who regularly supplied meat to Paris restaurants and had a farm in Calvados. The efficiency of the black market ensured that good meals could be had if one had the means. Whatever rationing system was in place before the liberation of Paris, I suspect, continued well after the war. My guess is that the dinner started off with a hearty soup, as all good French meals in a restaurant must. There was likely chicken or whatever was available from the countryside and if they were lucky, plenty of fresh vegetables would have made their appearance. Red wine would have been in abundance, perhaps the owner of the establishment would have surfaced a special vintage, one that had somehow escaped the scrutiny of German authorities. A small selection of French cheeses, again all from the countryside and for dessert there might even have been some fruit, or some little cakes perhaps baked on the premises. It mattered not what was or was not on the dining table, what was important was coming together and sharing this uniquely American tradition with friends and comrades because who knew what tomorrow might bring?

The Last Breakfast in Paris

I was recently asked a most ghastly question: When in Paris, where do you go for a real American breakfast? Trying valiantly not to be too flip, a good start would be for Madame to take the next plane to the U.S. would be a good start.

I am of two minds regarding best breakfast and Paris. I know plenty of my compatriots have searched high and low in the City of Lights for a place like home that will serve real breakfasts, you know, American-style breakfasts. For many it's a way of clinging to their roots in a strange town full of people who don't speak "real" American. I will lay my cards down, dear readers and state that I have simply no, and I mean that quite emphatically, no interest in wolfing down an American-style breakfast (read: largess) alone or while cornered at a table with my beloved compatriots in Paris. Call me finicky. You can shoot me now or perhaps later, after breakfast. If truth be told, arguably the best place to have your last breakfast in Paris is in bed. *Merci.*

I have always held the notion that the French are not ones to go "hog-wild" for *le* breakfast; it remains something of a mild curiosity that *les Americains* would want to indulge in a monumental meal before nine in the morning! *Les* French seem to me quite happy with a yogurt, a croissant or brioche. If you add *une petite amie* into the equation, you'll have all the ingredients for a very romantic French breakfast. Some would argue that in itself constitutes a regular *petit dejeuner*. Another story altogether.

Allow me to strap on my feed bag before proceeding further. Let's face it, we Yanks like, no, love, the thought of Big Breakfasts, it brings out that Paul Bunyan in all of us, the flannel shirts, wool cap and boots to be sure and standing ten feet tall. Survival of the fittest, full stomach and ready to conquer the world or maybe just the Mall of the Americas. The American breakfast is a classic among classics. It never ceases to amaze me that we continually insist on having that proverbial dump truck pull up to our plates and unload a ghastly combination of foods all generously lacquered with home-style maple syrup. You know I'm not that far from the horrible truth. We need to admit that. It is a first step.

Pull off the freeway and stop at any dinner or "greasy spoon" slide into that booth or perch yourself on the red Naugahyde stool that goes round-n-round, because you are about to enter into a culinary twilight zone. Miss Mabel, you know the one with the little pink hat and matching apron with those comfy white institutional crepe shoes. She'll be right with you "Hunn." Yes, Mabel with the voice that screams "two pack-a-day/shot o' Jack" will gladly recite the menu, flapjacks, or waffles (four or six) with or without two or four eggs, with or without ham, scrapple (a mush of pork scraps and trimmings);steak and bacon, two rolls and a pad of butter. No substitution please! Now, will that be with or without fries and gravy on the side? Or would you prefer hash browns or grits? It's a proud moment indeed when your order arrives; your arteries will stand up and give Mabel a "high five" because this is what we mean when we say, "Breakfast is ready in America!" Do not try and convince me otherwise. No "little" pot of jam along with a strange selection of breads and a cup of coffee with a handle that's smaller than my thumb can ever be considered a real breakfast! That's fine for Barbie and Ken. But not for me.

I am going to go out on that proverbial limb, once again, and suggest that there is not a live body anywhere in the good ol' USA who has not thoroughly enjoyed, at one time or another, a heaping power breakfast. The kind of breakfast that leaves your body stunned! It's a 9-11 breakfast for obvious reasons. But who cares? It is as American as standing in line on the boardwalk in 110 degrees to buy a bucket of greasy fries or a Pennsylvania Dutch creation the size of a flying saucer smothered in powdered sugar or maybe just a soft pretzel the size of a coiled boa constrictor, lathered in Mr. Yellow Mustard and all washed down with a gallon of some syrupy soft drink. I can assure you; you won't ever catch me doing that! Ever again.

The positive news is that having an American breakfast at an all-night diner somewhere off Route 66 at five o'clock in the morning or ten o'clock at night will not cost you anywhere near the price of an American breakfast served in a Paris local that has about as much Gallic charm as Euro Disney.

From the Little Coffee Pot, Naugahyde roadside heaven, Flo and Mabel are at your service, I return to the question of where to find that quintessential American breakfast in Paree. I dialed up a few of my connections – still friends -who seem to me to have a better pulse on these things and more tolerance than yours truly. No question about it, they would run to *Joe Allen*, the *Indiana I, The Real McCoy* or *Breakfast in America*. Now, I am no Inspector Clouseau, but there seems to be something of a discernible pattern in their suggestions. In the end I made two very reasonable suggestions: One was *"L'Américain"* a breakfast served at the Hôtel Plaza Athénée on the Avenue Montaigne where one can very nicely load up on pounds of eggs any style you want and just keep 'em coming. I am sure they have hot sauce as well. All for the moderate price of fifty-five euros. I recognized this might seem a bit pricey so going out of my way, I made another suggestion. Over on the Avenue George V you can get a much better deal at the Hotel George V. There they have an American-style breakfast to beat the band. Fresh juice, cereals, eggs any style and chocolate croissant! All for fifty-one euros. Much cheaper. They speak American too! The beauty of this location, of course, is that afterwards you can stop in next door at the American Cathedral to atone for your culinary sins, perhaps even to sleep.

If it's your last day in Paris, have breakfast in bed. *C'est plus facile* and more fun!

Why I Left Paris (Because Things Inevitably Get Complicated)

The canvas sky was deep blue with only a few well-placed cotton balls painted here and there seemingly haphazardly yet quite orderly at the same time. The puffy clouds would eventually drift off my canvas only to be followed by yet another set and then another. The Azure sky was a perfect match for the brilliant color of the Mediterranean. They could have been twins playing off each other. The Bay of Angels or *Baie des Anges* was beautiful and quiet in the early morning with only a small but brightly colored fishing boat some distance away hugging the horizon as it doggedly chugged along perhaps towards some secret fishing spot. Following the little boat was a small army of seagulls determined to be the first ones for a morning feeding. Much closer in, miniature waves lapped gently onto the rocky beach. There, a little boy urged his sailboat along the imaginary high seas as his mother looked on, contently, from her beach chair.

This particular morning found me sitting on a well-worn bench along the *Quai des Etas Unis*. Normally I would have been enjoying the peacefulness of the ocean view. But this time, I had my back turned away from the sea and facing one particular building with its many multicolored apartments, each with a view of the ocean. Even though it was *"hors de saison"* or the off season for tourists, many apartments still had their little shutters partially opened out taking full advantage of any passing ocean breezes. On one balcony there was a little dog on a mission to repeatedly yap at something, anything and that lasted until a tee-shirted man holding his morning paper rolled-up in one hand stepped out, waving his paper in the air, and grunting harshly. The barking stopped then resumed. On another brightly painted balcony, laundry had been placed outside to dry in the fresh air and along the rail, potted flowers of assorted colors were enjoying their time in the morning sun.

My gaze had fixed on one particular apartment on the third floor with its shutters firmly shut and a balcony empty of tables and chairs, its owners having clearly departed. I stared intently at it for a moment as if I could try and see inside then closed my eyes. I vividly recalled, as if it were yesterday, the living room with its French windows always open, curtains gently moving in the breeze and a glorious view of the *Baie des Anges* and the *Promenade des Anglais* hugging the bay as it wound gently around. I could see her clearly, standing by the window looking out pensively as she frequently did, smoking her favorite American cigarettes. Then she would turn away from the ocean view, gaze at me as if it were for the last time yet still wanting to believe I would return as I promised.

I had let nostalgia slowly creep over me, something I do increasingly these days or so it seems, reminding me of a time now long gone. So much had happened since then, yet it felt just like yesterday. You see, at that time I had reassured my book editor in Paris that what I really needed to get those great creative juices flowing again was a change of scenery, a change from the craziness of Paris. I assured him I would promptly deliver two chapters before my departure from Nice and not to worry. To paraphrase Robert Burns, the best laid plans of mice and men often go awry. In my case, indeed they did. But I am getting ahead of myself.

That winter in Paris had started off by being just plain awful or better yet, frightful, as my father was so fond of saying. As we turned the corner into the New Year, the ghastly (another favorite word) weather showed no signs of letting up. Gone were the festive decorations adorning the Champs d' Elysée and all the marketing that bombarded us with tested slogans and platitudes for a healthy and prosperous new year had also come and gone. We were now in the dark days where good mood and good cheer were replaced with icy sidewalks and chilly winds, the kind of winds that swept down the broad boulevards and avenues. Riding the mixing bowl of humanity, otherwise known as the Paris metro, one's senses were assaulted by the smell of stale tobacco, or someone's cheap perfume, residual garlic, and wet wool among others. The Paris sky had that forever threatening, unwelcoming gunmetal grey look to it. Thoughts of spring ever showing its face seemed more like a cruel joke despite the perky little *"meteo"* weather lady on one channel who kept chirping away incessantly that, oh yes, spring was in the air. Just wait and see, it's right around the corner! As far as I was concerned, my mood or just everything in my life seemed to mirror the weather. Lousy, bleak, and dark. I was not a happy camper, not even in Paris.

It was after one too many Pastis or one too many cognacs that it really hit me. What I needed was a vacation away from everything that seemed to contribute to my dark mood. Quite frankly, I felt it was something that was long overdue. Unfortunately, what I felt I needed rarely, if ever, meshed with the needs of my boss and my editor for life, two curmudgeons if I ever there were ones. Not like me you understand, the very embodiment of charm, wit, and diplomacy. You see what I do, in case you're remotely interested, is I report on special interest stories that can range from murders involving the very rich to stories on the impact of the arrival of a Tour de France *étape* on a small town in Brittany. And anything in between that strikes my fancy. Of course, convincing my editor remains an ever-constant hurdle. I also like to write in my spare time. How weird is that? It's a little bit like a busman's holiday. Our offices have always been in Paris and on the Left Bank, just a few feet away from the *Librairie Polonaise* on the *boulevard Saint-Germain*. It is not exactly what I would call luxury office space and it's tight but with four grumpy people and a part-time receptionist we somehow make do without anyone getting killed. We're on the third floor so we have quite a good view of the street below especially during the *manifestations* which seem to take place with greater and greater frequency on one issue more absurd then the next. I'm trying to be gentle here so don't get me wrong, freedom of speech is a fine thing I just don't like it interfering with my little daily habits. Oddly enough, we don't see too many demonstrations in the winter. How very strange.

On the bright side, one of the aspects about our office location that I find particularly appealing is that its location is midway between *Le Procope* at the one end and the Café de Flore at the other. So, if you were a writer, of sorts, then literary inspiration from either of these two famous Café's would be served up in heaping platters. For my meals, I usually suffered with a Croque Monsieur for lunch with perhaps a glass or two of wine, while for dinner I faced the difficult decision of choosing between cooking something at home or force myself to eat out and choosing among such exciting options as a nice Coq au Vin, one of my favorites, or perhaps even better, a *Tête de Veau* or a *Blanquette*. A delicious meal, a little wine, and some writing, then some cognac and coffee and little more writing. A perfect recipe for a great evening.

I hang my hat in a little apartment, also on the Left Bank, on the Boulevard Saint-Michel, a lovely tree-lined boulevard especially when Spring arrives. I was literally steps away from a respectable bistro and few cafes, a pizza joint, a Vietnamese restaurant, bookstores, and shops. It was ideal for me. I had picked-up the lease from one of our team members who was leaving on an extended assignment. Timing in this business is everything and you learn to pounce on these kinds of opportunities. Do not get the wrong idea that I somehow just waltzed my derriere in and set up camp. Remember there is nothing "easy" in France when it involves the long arm of government administration. I suspect if one dies in bed, it's only after proper documentation is signed and sealed then registered with the Marie. One's passing, therefore, is subject to prior approval so you want to make sure you get your papers in as early as possible. With any aspect of real estate, one must be prepared for the horrors of maneuvering through the bureaucratic maze that is passed off in France as efficiency. There is an unhealthy need for over-documentation and the French system has a unique way of grinding you and everyone else into bureaucratic submission. You have to experience the joys of working through the system to fully understand what I mean. As impatient a person as I am, it's like putting a gun to my head! From the French Government's perspective if you are unable to maneuver through their byzantine system of administration well, then maybe you don't deserve to get whatever it was that made you pull your hair and grind your teeth. When you think about it, there is some upside-down sense to this "folie."

I forgot to mention that I am on the fourth floor, so I have the option of walking up winding marble stairs or waiting patiently for a creaky elevator that was quite fashionable in my parents' heyday or perhaps when the Germans were visiting. When you are holding bags of groceries and balancing your briefcase waiting for the elevator to decide what it wants to do, all sorts of thoughts naturally run through your head, and I must admit that none of them are very pretty. My living room is decorated with comfortable furniture that one can actually use. There are lovely hardwood floors, of course, and a fireplace that I was told was decorative meaning it looks good and that's about it; no roasting marshmallows for me late in the evening. Interestingly enough, my bathroom (le WC) has a window that opens up and you can see the neighbors. I have waived a few times but no response as yet. My kitchen is a little strange, narrow but functional and well equipped which allows me to play a famously unknown French chef in my idle hours. I have a refrigerator with a freezer and a washer and dryer combo all in the same location. I found it confusing, and one time actually misplaced a leg of lamb only to find it in the washing machine. I blamed that entirely on the washing machine masquerading as a refrigerator. Cognac was not an issue, I assure you.

Was I leading a hermit's life? Did I miss someone meaningful in my life, beyond well, something short-short term? Let me be honest, sure I did but my life has been and still is a little crazy having to always run off as I do in search of a story in one part of the world or another. It was a life that was not relationship friendly or, so I was told more than just a few times. I thought about getting an animal. I hated cats because I do but I have always loved dogs but could not very well see myself having a pooch of some consequence that was at least bigger than some of the shoe boxes on a leash I see all too often. So, the case is closed.

On my free time, I am struggling with authoring the great American novel. Not really, actually it's more a collection of short stories but I'm working with an editor here in Paris who is not French but seems to have lived in Paris forever. Actually, I think he may be from Hungary or someplace like that of some nobility as well and for some strange reason he's taken a shine to my story, my angle on life and the different lenses through which I am able to view the world.

I'm facing writer's block these days. It's what every writer faces at some point. It's the brick wall that you can't seem to tear down not even with insane alcohol treatments, meaningless interludes, or overindulgence in anything else that might come to mind. The wall remains. That is when the idea of a vacation struck me as being the first sensible idea I've have in a long time. I thought about hopping a train down to the south of France, finding someplace to hold up and losing myself for a while. Maybe I would call my office maybe not. Fresh air and a change of scenery are always the first things people suggest that I do especially with the French. Fresh air is especially important and a trip to the country are both very important. It could be key to breaking through my writing bloc and actually move forward. I had convinced myself but when I told my boss that I needed time away, he snorted disagreeably, blew his nose then muttered something about not taking too long and a lot of people would just die to have my job and on and on heaping the guilt on me. Likewise, my Hungarian editor looked at me as if I had two heads and disagreed with me flat out reminding me that I was not a young man anymore. Running away was not the answer, I should come to my senses. All in all, it was not the bon voyage sendoff I had hoped for.

I arrived late afternoon at the Gare de Nice Ville after a re-markably uneventful five and half hour trip from Paris, Gare de Lyon as my train wound slowly wound its way down to the south of France. Second thoughts of my having made a giant mistake gradually dissipated and I was starting to actually feel a little more alive and yes, dare I say, excited. Before leaving Paris, I placed a call to an old friend, Principal Inspector Lambert now retired from the Antibes-Juan-les-Pins police department. At the time, I was following an interesting case involving a brutal murder of a hedge fund mogul and I recalled my headline ran "Hedge Fund Mogul Found Dead, Brutally Beaten in Villa – by Special Correspondent..." The local paper Nice Matin called it quite simply "Une Sale Affair." In any event, Inspector Lambert just happened to have a one-bedroom rental available on the Rue du Paradis. Three flights up. Instructions were given where to find the key. I was set.

TOWARDS THE COTE D'AZUR

A Tasty *Bouchon* Lyonnais

" *Chez M'man*" is located very near the *Place Bellecour* on the *rue des Maronniers*. You will know that you are on the right track because the street has one little *bouchon* (petit restaurant) after another. Everyone is doing just what you are doing. Reading one prix fixe menu after another and trying to decide what suits their taste on this particular evening or their meager expense account. When everything looks good it a difficult challenge.

In Lyon, nose-to-tail dining, as colorful as it sounds, means devouring the entire animal the way they've been doing it for centuries. And arguably, the best place to sample this type of cuisine is at one of the city's many "*bouchons*," small restaurants serving simple, hearty dishes with ingredient lists that can sound like an anatomy lesson. Typical foods include *andouille* (grilled chitterlings sausage), tripe (pig or cow's stomach), or *boudin noir* (blood sausage). Other more recognizable dishes include, chicken liver salad, *Cerverlas,* (raw pork sausages,) *Quenelles* (flour, egg, and cream dumplings), or *Cervelle de canut,* (which means "brains of the silk-weaver" and consists of cream cheese mixed with garlic and chives.) Some of the contemporary *bouchons* serve more upscale French cuisine, such as foie gras and truffles, but for many *Lyonnais,* true *bouchons* such as this one, the house strives to only offer foods that are distinctly unpretentious. With that in mind off I went in search of traditional *bouchon* cooking. And did I ever find it!

Chez M'man is a hub of activity, and it gets even busier as the evening progresses and louder as the wine flows. The super friendly waiter ushered me to a table facing a huge chalkboard on the wall listing all the menu items. How convenient. He then took my order scribbling it down on a piece of butcher paper then promptly stuck it under my paper tablecloth. It's clearly an art form and a style that I was unaware of. With a sense of duty and honor he quickly reappears with a breadbasket and my bottle of Beaujolais. What a life saver! Within seconds the cork was out, and the wine presented for tasting. I do love good service. I must note that they had an interesting concept of interior decoration which consisted of stoves of various shapes and sizes (yes, that's right, stoves) hanging upside down from the ceiling. If you have good life insurance there's nothing to be worried about.

I carefully perused the menu. I could go with a *Salade Lyonnaise* or *Salad Savoyarde,* the chicken liver salad or perhaps a cold ratatouille. I took aim and started with *l'assiette de M'man* which arrived in a round dish with thick slices of cured pork Lyonnaise sausage cooked in a goose liver-based soufflé also known as a *gâteau de foies*. I will admit that by the time I finished this "light" dish, one or two pieces of bread with creamy butter and not too surprisingly, half a bottle of Beaujolais, I could have stopped there. Some of you may come to learn that once I start, I am not one to shy away from a gastronomical challenge. N*on, cela n'ai pas permi* – at least in my book. Onward I went deeper into the belly of the beast. I did not have far to think about. The challenge was right before my eyes: *Boudin Noir* a la Lyonnaise – a specialty of Lyonnaise cooking. It might as well have been screaming my name. I polished off the remains of the bottle and quickly ordered just a half-bottle of Beaujolais. I am a man with limits after all.

I did not have long to wait. My waiter reappeared tableside and with a flourish placed the plate before me. I looked at my plate, blinked then looked again only to realize I recognized absolutely nothing on my plate! What foolish thing had I done? I asked my waiter for a cheat sheet on my chosen dish. Politely he pointed that I would be eating *Andouillets* which is a coarse-grained sausage made with pork, intestines, pepper, wine, onions, and other seasonings. The breaded piece to the right of the sausage, Monsieur, was none other than *Gratin de tripe a l'ancienne* or a piece of breaded tripe which is the lining of the cow. Of course, how silly of me not know that ! And last but not least, the *piece de resistance*, itself, the very *boudin noir* or blood sausage. If it's good enough for the French Foreign Legion to sing about, then my goodness it's good enough for me! All three were different and all surprisingly tasty. The tripe was a bit chewy shall we say but tasty. This was a quintessentially Lyonnais dish, so I really had no other choice.

To close out the evening, I had the Saint *Marcellin* which is a soft cow's milk cheese and quite delicious.

By the way, don't expect to pull out your AmEx card and presume it will be graciously accepted. No way. The AmEx card, it seems, is less and less welcome around these parts. Asia, it's a different story as they kill to get your business and the card. Better off with using a Visa or the Carte Bleue Visa. Just a friendly reminder.

I rolled out into the street and proceeded to retrace my steps to my favorite hotel. Perhaps a Cognac outside under the heated lamps and observe the *vas-et-vient* of the *beau monde*, or perhaps to sleep?

DINER IN THE GARDEN OF FRANCE (FRICASSÉE DE VOLAILLE AU VOUVRAY)

'Thence a valley opens down to the Loire, from Montvazon at the head; the hills seem to rebound under the country-houses on each of the slopes; it is a glorious emerald basin, and at the bottom the Indre winds in serpentine curves'.

— Honoré de Balzac (1799-1850) An extract from Le Lys dans la Vallée

In the Loire Valley, it's hard to avoid coming face to face with the beauty and majesty of French history. The region, the people, the food and wine, the culture and its history are all so richly intertwined as one. It's not at all difficult to feel as if you could easily slip away into another time. The Loire Valley is the embodiment of French history, and you find it at every turn and it's all but inevitable that at some point, somewhere, the richness of the Loire Valley's past will reach out and grab you and never let you go. If it's not the story of *Jeanne d'Arc,* it's the beauty of the Renaissance, or perhaps the magnificent *châteaux's* that seem to dot the landscape at every turn. One or all of these will surely capture your fancy. The region is home to such well-known names as *Chambord, Bourges, Amboise* and *Blois*, favorite residences of French Kings and Queens from the Middle Ages to the Renaissance; house-hold names like Louis XII, *François* I, *Henri* II, and *Catherine de Medici* are but examples of those who would call the Loire Valley, their home. But beyond kings and queens, the Loire Valley has also inspired some great artists and big thinkers – from *Honoré de Balzac* and Leonardo da Vinci to *Georges Sand* and *Rene Descartes*. It's all about the richness of history and a richness that has indeed blessed this garden of France.

Let me pose a simple question: What do *Muscadet, Sancerre, Chinon, Bourgueil,* and a nicely chilled *Pouilly-Fumé* possibly all have in common with *Rillettes, Crottin de Chavignol,* potted rabbit, a *fricassée* of chicken cooked in white wine from *Anjou,* partridge with wild mushrooms or perhaps pork medallions cooked with prunes, cream, and white wine? If your answer was: "Typical foods found along the Atlantic City boardwalk" then you are most certainly wrong. The correct answer would be that these are just some examples of the traditional food and wine selections from the Loire Valley, home to outstanding grape va-rietals and regional foods that will have you coming back and begging for more.

Little known factoid for cocktail conversation over peanuts and Scotch: Did you know that the Loire is the longest river in France, and the wine appellations that stretch along it, from the Atlantic Coast to the center of the country, produces more white wine than any other region in France?

Can you imagine a cornucopia of white wines, plenty to drink for everyone! That's Heaven and maybe it's not in Iowa. Clearly, I have a thing going with wines from the Loire Valley and not the least bit ashamed to admit it. I am proud of it. I have long suggested or at least made strong references to the pure enjoyment of drinking a *Chinon* or a *Bourgueil.* They are usually on the wine hit list in many a Paris bistro because it's simple, elegant, light, tasty and pairs with so many dishes. Enough said and will descent from my soapbox.

I had some difficulty in selecting a dish that would not only reflect the region but be tasty and do-able in the sense that readers would not be put off by it's difficult or complexity or that it would require far too much prep time. One of my goals has always been to discuss good French food and wine in the context of its locality in France. That way it is a pleasant mix of learning something new with something delicious. I hope that is understood and found useful. With that in mind, I have selected a little dish that will let you begin your trip to the Loire Valley. Always start on a full stomach, much like Napoleon's grenadiers. Please enjoy!

This is a wonderful dish (found in the recipe selection at the end) and is made with free-range chickens and rich, white *Vouvray* wine. Adapted from a recipe by *Chef Francois Salle* when he was at the *Auberge de la Brenne*, just a few miles from the heart of the *Vouvray* wine-growing region. The restaurant offers the very best of the culinary traditions and fine produce of the *Touraine* region. Dishes like sausage and shallot tart and rabbit delicately stewed in a *sauvignon* sauce. Be still my heart.

A MEMORABLE DINNER IN THE LANGUEDOC-ROUSSILLON

*T*ucked away in the 12th Century fortified village of *Rivesaltes* at 11 Rue Armand Barbès and just beneath the imposing church and bell tower is a wonderful little hotel/restaurant appropriately named *"La Tour de l'Horloge"* owned and operated by Monsieur et Madame Bercie a delightful couple who pride themselves on their hospitality and especially their cuisine which is both *"authentique et régionale."* It was all that and so much more as I soon found out. But first let me set the scene.

I was on a business trip heading from Barcelona to Montpellier, a trip that takes a little over three hours by car as one dodges the super-sized *camions* and the usual crazy drivers whizzing past in their sleek high-priced engines at a conservative 160-180 km/hr. All I saw was the blur and all I heard were the sound of repeated horns being leaned on in a massive display of European exasperation.

Thinking ahead, I had leased a nice Peugeot equipped with more bells and whistles than I ever knew what to do with and more importantly a GPS as I am famous for getting lost even in my own bedroom. The idea was a good one, but in practice I soon found the voice of the electronic British "marm" drilling incessantly into my head more than just annoying and I was soon ready to bash the system and her electronic voice to bits. Cruel and unjust you say? Her directions were poor in many instances, "in two hundred meters, at the next roundabout, take the 4th exit then proceed for two hundred meters and take the first left." There would be a pause then "at the next opportunity make a U turn then proceed three hundred meters." When you're counting roundabout exits and listening to someone who has NO business speaking French while dodging the *camions* and crazy traffic, I need something I can count on. She clearly had failed me and failed me repeatedly. I won't even go into where she led me but on the plus side, I did get to see some interesting parts of town. I later complained vociferously to the rental agency in Barcelona. They nodded and agreed to take her off my bill forever. Another crazy American!

Following a quick stay in Montpellier and an unremarkable dinner except for the wine, my next stop was to be in the town of Perpignan proper but as luck would have it, the powers at be had me going somewhere outside of the city in one of those French brand name hotels that are efficient and streamlined and completely and utterly void of warmth and charm or even a good French meal for that matter. As I said, they are efficient and economical and market research must show that for French families on the move especially for their never-ending holidays, this is just what Papa et *Maman* desire. I want to go on record as stating that they are simply the worst and should be banned from this earth for all times. I actually did spend one night at this same brand name hotel in another part of the world but at a their higher-end hotels. They did have a small cocktail lounge which was their only saving grace. My room was so efficiently laid out there was no room to even change my mind. Awful I say, simply awful. Have I made my point?

Once installed in my college dorm room, I scanned the internet for an escape route and a good meal and discovered that the little village of *Rivesaltes* was within minutes from my place of incarceration.

The fortified village of *Rivesaltes* is deep in the heart of the vineyards of the Roussillon, famous for its Muscat-sec and close to the river *Agly* and and just 10 klicks from the Mediterranean Sea (*Port Barcares*). Now some of you may be interested in knowing that the town of *Rivesaltes* is also the birthplace of General Joffre, a famous World War I French hero (remember Papa Joffre?) His name is also attached to an internment camp which has a sordid and painful history during the Second World War. It served as a transit camp for deportees whose ultimate destination would be the Nazi extermination camps. I decided to drive past the remains of the camp as I was sufficiently intrigued to see just what was left of the camp. The only other internment camp I have ever seen or visited was Camp Breendonk which is just outside of Antwerp in Willebroek.

There I was alone on a lonely and narrow stretch of a well-worn road facing what remained of Camp Rivesaltes or Camp Joffre. On either side of me were the remains of what had likely been prisoner housing. The very same housing that years before had welcomed soldiers fleeing Franco's Civil War. Looking around it was hard not to be moved, saddened to think about the sure and certain fate of the Jews who would inevitably be shipped to German death camps. While I had no wish to reach back into the recesses of my mind, I thought about those who had also been sent from Germany in 1940 to a similar internment camp, located in Gurs, in southwest France. In particular, my paternal great grandmother Helena (my paternal aunt's name) who I literally knew nothing of or about including the family and what I knew I learned though persistent research, having gone down many a rabbit hole and eventually connecting with far distant relatives living in Germany. As I was led to understand, Helena's forced departure at the age 90 to the Gurs Internment Camp was never accomplished as she died in the trains somewhere along the journey and her body eventually disposed of prior to or on arrival at the camp. I shuttered thinking about the story and wishing that it had not bubbled up from somewhere deep inside me. I returned to my car and slowly drove back and met my colleague and planned our dinner.

On this lovely late afternoon in June, the town was very quiet. The only things that seemed to be moving were kids with their soccer balls and a few wandering tourists. Walking the narrow streets, I marveled at the history of this place and quite sure that little had changed in so many years. On rare exceptions I had to move on to the sidewalk to avoid being run over by a car determined to speed by yet barely fitting on the narrow road. I discovered, quite by accident, the center of town marked by the only café in town and of course one bakery. Let's remember where we are! I found myself quite clearly at the very epicenter of the village. A few old men were gathered at a table enjoying the shade of an equally old tree, while other customers like myself, who were not so lucky, felt the heat of the Mediterranean sun despite the cover afforded by a pale green stripped awning. With the help of a few cold "Pression's" (beer on tap), I suffered through as the sun slowly faded behind the church tower. Wondering if a restaurant existed, I turned to the inevitable source of all information, *Madame la Propriétaire* who was inside meticulously wiping and re-wiping her zinc counter. We chatted about the weather, tourists, and business and then I asked her about a place to eat. This is the sort of question that is most important to the French.

Recommendations are not just given lightly, "take a left Bud and there's your sandwich joint." *Non, pas du-tout*, Madame pondered the question carefully for a minute then told me there were only two restaurants she could really suggest. The Clock Tower Hotel noted for its Catalan food. She started with the directions then stopped and said, "come with me I will show you myself." Off we went down one street and another finally she pointed "one more block then make your right Monsieur."

I made a command decision and headed off in the direction of the Clock Tower Hotel which I had passed during my wanderings. What drew me to this restaurant was the promise of good

Catalan cooking something that I am very fond of and difficult to find. Just what is Catalan cooking you may well ask? It brings Spain and the Basque together with the Languedoc-Roussillon region. It leans heavily on fresh vegetables especially tomatoes, eggplant, and garlic and olive oil, beans and mushrooms, ham, tuna, anchovies, and incredible cheeses. It is a little bit of heaven.

The owner, who I later found out was also the chef, sat me down in a little courtyard area with palm trees set against massive rock walls. He suggested that I try the local *Muscat-sec* while I perused the menu. I am not a particular fan of *Muscat* and find it's never quite *sec* (dry) enough – at least for me. I tasted and thanked him and promptly ordered a nice bottle of local Languedoc red. I was much happier. Don't toy with me when it comes to such serious matters. For starters, I have to tell you, I was torn between having *moules* (mussels) in aioli or *soupe de poisson* (fish soup.) I opted for the latter and it arrived *a table* in a hefty tureen with a large dollop the size of an iceberg of aioli floating on top; a side of crispy garlic toasts complemented the soup quite well. Was it good? It was incredible, no I mean really incredible where you lick your lips with every taste and find yourself mopping up every last bit of soup with crunchy bread *du pays*. I could have stopped there. But with another glass of red, it was time to really get serious. I asked the owner, and by now we were best friends, for his suggestions which he gladly volunteered. He paused, as if preparing to offer a very serious recommendation, since I was going Catalan, he stated, I should have the *Boles de Picoulat* (*spécialité Catalane*) at least it was so stated on the menu. The dish was an interesting and delightful mixture of medium size pieces of pork and beef meatballs in a thick and very rich red sauce on top of a cream base. Soon you find yourself knee-deep in this rich, spicy creamy heavenly *mélange*. After a few more glasses of wine (who's counting anyway) and some strong black coffee, I found I had room for absolutely nothing more except maybe a little desert. Good food is serious business. Not too much mind you, just a little something. There was one and only thing that caught my eye, the *Crème Catalane*. No arms need be twisted, and I volunteered to take one for the team. This little desert takes the *Crème Caramel*, we all know and love, to a whole other level. We are talking doctoral studies ladies and gentlemen. Yes, that kind of level. It was perfectly done, the burnt caramel done just right, and each spoonful of that rich, sweet, eggy mixture was bringing me closer to a state of perpetual bliss.

It's hard to forget culinary experiences like that especially with such charming hosts. I thoroughly enjoyed myself and cannot wait to plan for my return. In the meantime, I get to look forward to making my way back to Barcelona airport and my GPS ride from Hell.

BLACK TRUFFLE HUNTING I GO

I am fascinated by truffles and sure that I am not alone in that respect. I have always wanted to go truffle hunting that is, in part because it has always held some mystique, a secret known but to handful of truffle hunters and secondly, I wanted to try my new shotgun which they said I would need because truffles are quick on their feet. I knew that truffle hunting secrets and family secrets are sometimes one and the same.

Most truffle hunting secrets are passed on from generation to generation, from one death bed to another undoubtedly. Asking for tip on hunting the black truffle of Périgord is much like asking a Chef what makes for that special something in the sauce. The Chef, ever polite, will gladly oblige but may forget an ingredient or two. A secret is a secret *mon ami.*

Some years ago, I was fairly sure a truffle was a wonderful and delicious chocolate miracle rolled in powdered cocoa and when tasted came pretty darn close to what I thought was Nirvana. Yes, that was state of heavenly bliss and I for one was quite content to have found it at last. That was then. I had packed my shotgun in anticipation of going truffle hunting. I am excited.

The white and black truffle is a fungal fruiting body that develops underground and relies on microphage for spore dispersal. Almost all truffles are fungi and therefore usually found in close association with trees. The white truffle or Alba madonna (*Tuber magnatum*) comes from the Langhe area of the Piedmont region in northern Italy and, most famously, in the countryside around the city of Alba. The black truffle or the winter black Périgord truffle (*Tuber melanosporum*) is named after the Périgord region in France and grows exclusively with oak. Specimens can be found in late autumn and winter, reaching 7 cm in diameter, and weighing up to 100 g. The 18th-century French gastronome Brillat-Savarin called these truffles *"the diamond of the kitchen"* then went on to note that *the truffle is not exactly an aphrodisiac, but it tends to make women more tender and men more likeable."*

Somewhat earlier, a learned gentlemen by the name of Cicero considered the truffle as *"children of the earth."* That says a little bit about how long truffles have been in our hearts, minds and stomachs. The largest truffle market in France (and probably also in the world) is at Richerenches in Vaucluse. The largest truffle market in southwest France is at Lalbenque in Quercy. These markets are busiest in the month of January, when the black truffles have their highest perfume. Black truffles were recently sold for about $1,000 a pound in a farmer's market and twice that retail. Hardly what you would call dirt cheap.

Total annual European production has dipped considerably from 2,000 tons at the end of the 19th century to just 60 tons a few seasons back. Why the decline? A loss of interest? No, blame it on woods gone wild, a result of the population fleeing from the countryside (truffles need a light, airy environment) and unusual weather patterns. Some worry that if the trend continues, the French truffles could disappear altogether. This could mean war. Can you imagine armies lining up on their respective borders (all waving their Covid-10 passports of course) then charging, let's say into Italy (because it makes more sense that way) and laying claim to the white truffles of Piedmont. The Great Truffle War. It could happen.

Gaston and his wife Lisette run a small side business, deep in Périgord's black truffle country, catering to smart aleck tourists like me who think they know a little too much for their own good and usually end up in trouble. Point well taken. The business of pandering to tourists is relatively new to them but since a number of English mom and pop operations have sprung up, they have decided to do the real thing; and good for them too. Gaston met me out in the courtyard of his ancestral farmhouse at 7:00 AM sharp. He had been up hours before and Lisette had been busy cooking since, well ever since I arrived, she seemed glued to the stove. Gaston was appropriately dressed in green twill pants, heavy farmer boots, flannel shirt, maroon colored wool sweater, tweed cap covering a shock of white hair, a ruddy complexion with a perennial cigarette pasted to the corner of his lower lip. Hand outstretched, his thick gnarly fingers looking more like carrots than human fingers, he grasped my hand which seemed to disappear from sight.

Et bien bonjour Monsieur, il fait beau ce matin.

He looked me over with a twinkle of amusement in his bright blue eyes, clearly, I was not exactly *du pays,* dressed as I was in a nice cashmere sweater, khaki pants and polo shirt and LL Bean leather mocks and leather jacket. I could pass for a native anywhere, I was sure of it and asked if we were riding in the red BMW 1-Series that I had rented at the airport ever anxious to show off what this baby could do on the open road, oh yea! Apparently the 1985 Citroen was going to do just fine instead. I got dressed for nothing!

Gaston opened the back door and whistled softly, and Carlo quickly appeared from somewhere in the kitchen looking just a bit guilty then proceeded to hop into the backseat. Carlo was a passenger of sorts, a *Lagotto Romagnolo* which is a breed of dog that comes from the Romagna sub-region of Italy. The name means "water dog from Romagna," coming from the Italian word lago, lake. Gaston explained that the breeds traditionally function as a gun dog, specifically as a water retriever. However, they are often used to hunt for truffles. And Carlo had already made a name for himself as a sharp-nosed black truffle hunter and someone to be taken quite seriously. He had these large, round dark yellow eyes, a thick curly woolly coat which was off-white with brown patches, cute enough, but perhaps not as cute as my dear Golden Retriever, Monsieur Louie.

On the way to our truffle hunting destination, Gaston explained that the female pig's natural truffle seeking, as well as her usual intent to eat the truffle, is due to a compound within the truffle similar to androstanol, the sex pheromone of boar saliva, to which the sow is keenly attracted. He laughed but clearly truffle eating pigs were a problem. Carlo on the other hand, did not have that problem. I asked Gaston about the market for truffles. He told me that he had heard from a reliable source that Chinese truffles worth no more than wild mushrooms that were doctored and sold as Périgord truffles. Apparently, they look just like Périgord truffles, so it's easy to get taken. He pulled out a bag and handed me what looked like a truffle; it smelled as I expected a fresh truffle to smell like.

"These are real ?" I asked.

"Ahhh, mais bien sûr que non Monsieur, c'est du Chinois !"

Dishonest dealers were putting genuine truffles among their Chinese mushrooms to pick up the aroma and pass the sniff test and then selling them to people, well like me who thought knew everything. That's downright underhanded I thought to myself.

So how does one know a real truffle from a fake truffle? Well from Gaston's School of Truffles, I learned there are a couple of things to keep in mind. Good truffles are harvested at the height of maturity and their aroma and taste after ten days is fleeting. So be sure and ask, "the little man" (it's always a little man, it seems) selling them at his stand when did they arrive or when were they picked. You also use the sniff test and if the strong pungent truffle smell is faint or non-existent, do like the song says, "just walk on by." Like all good things in France – of the food and drink varietal, truffles are regulated every which way but Sunday. To translate, truffles that are 1 to 1.4 ounces in size would be classified as an Extra Grade truffle. Truffles are graded Extra, Category 1, Category 2 and Unclassified. There are both weight and aesthetic considerations. Extra truffles must weigh a minimum of 30 grams and be the size of a ping-pong ball, with a similarly round shape; they must have "very slight" defects. If not, you're taken to truffle prison in Périgord's very own Bastille, kept in the dark and eventually you'll be let out with a few slight defects of your own.

Gaston's family has owned a piece of truffle land for a number of generations – not that long in truffle history time – but the land, the five acres, have been good and every year he has managed to make "a little money" and then some to put away. I did not doubt for one moment that his conservative temperament combined with the bounty of the land had indeed been good to both he and Lisette. True to form, Carlo was out the door in a heartbeat. I think he knew the drill, nose to the ground, it was a pleasure to watch. Soon enough, Gaston grinning, handed me a dark ugly, odd-shaped object and told me to smell and let him know if I thought it was real. It had an incredibly deep, pungent, earthy aroma to it. I had died and gone to heaven. I could have used a glass of red wine, perhaps some cheese with bits of freshly shaved truffle to better enjoy the sport of it all.

BREAKFAST IN VIEUX NICE AT *LE COIN QUOTIDIEN*

I had successfully completed yet another wonderful breakfast at *Le Coin Quotidien* my new "go to" haunt for breakfast. I find I will exhaust myself by repeatedly returning to the same *endroit* until such time as I have tried almost everything on the menu and can recite the menu from memory, staring with page one. A little bit of overkill going on here, you think? Perhaps my obsessiveness is oozing out. It happens.

In any event, I digress. The food *au Coin* was solid and the view worth every penny. I had my "usual" which consisted of a *Café Crème* served in a bowl, which took me back to another era, a glass of freshly pressed orange juice and an assortment of croissants and slices of country bread along with a delicious selections of jams including fig jam. What a delicious moment to be cherished! Maybe I had the same breakfast yesterday. I forget but it's my right.

Today, the Gods were favoring me, and I found an open table outside. The location here is wonderful, and I always enjoy the *vas-et-viens* the ebb and flow of the Flower Market located within steps of *Le Coin*. Little toy cars zip along the *rue Louis Gassin* only to disappear somewhere below ground. To be sure, there was a fine selection of visual distractions, locals dressed casually to impress and many walking their little so-called dogs. *Non merci,* not for *moi*. Of course, the gaggle of tourists who looked and acted like, well, like tourists were in plentiful supply. In fact, seated at a table next to me were six Russian women of various sizes but unfortunately none with the glamour of la Femme Nikita that many of us (OK me) hoped to meet someday, preferably just not in a dark alley. On this occasion, I felt badly for the poor waiter who was doing his very best to place the Russian's breakfast order. Clearly, he spoke no Russian and his English was delicate at best. The Russian gals, demonstrating all the fineness of a herd of elephants in a China shop, spoke no French or did not want to try and only spoke brutish English. At one point they became indignant demanding why they should have to pay for an additional breakfast serving when they were only six orders. Why? Why? Against my better judgement (*will I ever learn that no good deed*

goes unpunished?), I turned around and interjected in English telling the charming assembly that the waiter only wanted to know
if they would each like a plate on the side. *Spasibo,* or a thank you
would be appropriate. Amazing how languages can get so twisted
and convoluted from mouth to ear to the next. I received a surly
look for my efforts and if looks could kill. The waiter whispered
a hushed "*merci*" on the way by. Having finished my second coffee, I decided it was time to roam the flower market square and
seek out the inviting little side streets of Vieux Nice. There was
an open book market somewhere near that I wanted to uncover.
And you know, it's never too soon to start thinking about lunch.

Lunch in Vieux Nice at

Bistro d'Antoine

The restaurant is tucked away between the Rue Saint Reparate and the Rue Benoit Bunico at 27 rue de la Prefecture, easily "*une bonne address*" in vieux Nice. Now granted, not the easiest place to find especially for me who needs a GPS strapped to my side because I can get lost in my own bedroom. I would have been miserable had I missed my lunch reservation. That's one of the few smart things I did in Nice. Word to the wise, if you think you can charm your way into a seat, think again!

This truly is a delightful, authentic, and cozy French Bistro. This is not what you might call "haute cuisine" by any stretch of the imagination. Rather, it is good authentic Niçoise food. And for that I am eternally thankful. The service is both friendly and efficient. While I was there, you could have thrown a crouton in any direction and hit a tourist. That was the sad part but we all must make do these days.

The trouble with a really good restaurant where they know what they're doing is that it shows in spades and once again I find myself agonizing over the menu options on a chalkboard full of many regional favorites —beef salad with anchovy dressing, butter risotto with truffles, grilled calamari, sliced leg of lamb, *Magret de Canard* or duck breast, traditional pork casserole and boudin noir. You see what I mean? What to choose! One almost needs Biblical wisdom in choosing from the menu. I was all out of wisdom by noon anyway, biblical, or otherwise so I decided to start my adventure with a superb salad of squid and endives. Hard to go wrong when you marry squid and endives. I will pay premium price for endives because in a little homemade vinaigrette is something I truly enjoy, over and over again. But I digress.

For my main course I decided on the slow pot roasted pork shank in an incredible red wine reduction. This came with a pot of roasted local fresh vegetables from the market literally around the corner, of that I had no doubt. I prepared, steeled myself for my adventure with a little *amuse bouche* of sardine terrine and freshly cut baguette and pleasantly washed down with a lovely Rose de Provence. I get weak-kneed just writing this.

Out the window with Nouvelle Cuisine for now and let in the fresh Mediterranean air! It was a feast of the Gods and no denying that! Because I don't like sharing, I would grudgingly recommend this little bit of Heaven hands-down! Was I interested in a desert? Is the Pope Catholic? I opted for a delicious desert of fresh pineapple and mango with a ginger crumble mixed through it. Oh my, choosing well is indeed an art not a science and must be taken seriously. A little Martel cognac to join a coffee concluded this strenuous mid-day activity. I could only imagine what the evening would hold for me. I made my way through the narrow side streets to the *Promenade des Anglais,* Avenue of the English, bordering the peaceful vivid blue Mediterranean Sea then I briskly walked home enjoying a lovely November afternoon and completing my exercise for the week. Only a few hours before dinner, I had to be ready!

Le Cannet, the Chocolate Festival and Room for Dinner

Just what is a "Cannet" and why am I even going there in the first place? Good questions. Barely a week ago, I was in *Beaulieu-sur-Mer* recovering from a fishing expedition with my friend Luc, the crazy ex-paratrooper. Suffice to say it truly was an "expedition" and after a sumptuous feast, I felt I needed a week's bed rest. I eventually regained sufficient strength and contacted the *Marie du Cannet Côte D'Azur* hoping that someone in their *Tourisme, Hébergement et Restauration* Consular, tourist section could advise me on a modest hotel in town. I told the chirpy, efficient little voice on the other end of the line that I wanted a room in close proximity to *La Fête du Chocolat*. That's right folks a chocolate festival high in the hills!

To help you all get situated, Le Cannet is in the northern part of *la ville de Cannes* on the Cote d'Azur and the gorgeous Mediterranean. That is the same Cannes that is usually stuffed with movie stars with uber egos, glamorous hangers-on, high prices, swarms of *paparatzi*, bad attitudes, pushy eastern European tourists with too much money, all driving around in their Maserati's (rented.) If you're lucky you might even run into a real local who actually speaks French though I understand they are something of a dying breed.

A little family side note. Years ago, my maternal grandparents would take the family, my mother, brothers and sisters, and summer in the South of France. I mean, don't we all do that? If they weren't suffering too terribly much in *Villefranches*, they were renting a "little flat" in Le Cannet. My mother and her four siblings would walk along the *Croissette* in Cannes trying to spot famous actors and in fact, once saw Charlie Chaplain.

While my maternal grandparents were enjoying the Mediterranean, my paternal grandparents were spending their summers in Le Touquet-Paris, Plage in a lovely, rented villa. There was no end to their suffering.

For one reason or another, my sainted mother never lost her accent *du Midi* and as the polite well-behaved children that we were, laughed our heads off whenever my mother would pronounce certain words (*une rose* comes to mind) with the unmistakable accent "*du Midi*." As kids, we wondered in endless amazement why our mother could not pronounce here words in French like us, little Parisian smart-ass *voyous*, badly behaved, who knew just about everything there was worth knowing about. End of that story.

Le Cannet was originally part of Cannes but became a commune in 1778 after a crowd of early movie stars, expats, and retirees took to the streets in demonstrations; more than likely they were demanding better pay, less hours and *gaz à tous les étages* (gas at every floor.) The town is nestled in the heart of seven hills along a gentle slope with panoramic views of the surrounding countryside. In case you get lost, it's good to know that Cannet is divided into two areas – the old town (*vieux Cannet*) formerly the ancient village of *Castrum de Caneto* and is, as you might expect, rich with ambiance, cobbled streets with medieval buildings, interesting gateways, delicious little restaurants, the ruins of a chateau and the lovely St. Michel church where you can atone for your last nights' behavior. The newer part of town is the more commercial area and sure enough, you can't turn around without bumping into a tourist with a stupid guidebook and clearly one who is not a native of *Castrum de Caneto*. If you're into hiking, biking, horse-riding and fishing or if your seeking peace and quiet then Le Cannet is perfect especially if you've experienced enough of the hustle and bustle of Cannes, the red carpet, yet another festival for one insane reason or the other, the beautiful people, the sun worshipers, the loud and quite often rude pushy tourists with bad attitudes, waxen faces suntanned just right, too much money and dripping in gold from... well, I will let you hazard a guess.

To reach my destination from Cannes, one takes the *Boulevard Carnot* driving north out of town. Once you reach the *rond-point,* or the roundabout or the traffic circle, the road cleverly is renamed *Boulevard Sadi Carnot.* One small piece of critical information. If you happen to be driving something less than glitzy (as I normally do) say a well-used *deux Cheveaux* you are best advised to leave Cannes as early in the morning as possible so as not to be seen by the *glitteratzy.* Let me explain. Last year, and this is according to the *Nice-Matin,* that premier daily covering all the news from the southeast and Corsica that's fit to print, a couple from Moldova in their new-to-you 403 Peugeot, had the misfortune of leaving town during the daylight hours and were pelted with a shower of pebbles by a crowd of, what the *Matin* described as, beautifully well-dressed people. To add insult to injury, a *porte-parole* for the *Commissariat de Police de Cannes* or the Police public relations officer, commented on the incident by "shrugging" his shoulders and then promptly excusing himself to go to lunch. Get a Rolls Royce or leave town very early. You will thank me later.

Miss chirpy voice from the *Tourisme, Hébergement* was true to her word and arranged a stay for me a charming and quaint little hotel. I say quaint because they still used the *minuterie* system to efficiently manage their electricity. It's a twist on saving energy where certain lights are timed out, for example one's bathroom. In Paris, you find it in the hallways, stairwells, garages, and other places no one usually frequents. A word about the chocolate festival which is truly *"Le rendez-vous des gourmands"* and held at the end of March, 10:00 AM sharp! By the time you're starting to enjoy your first cup of coffee with the *Matin du Midi*, crowds are already gathering at the *Place Bellevue* and *rue Saint-Sauveur*. Chocolate-themed events are one of the few times where I do not let children get in my way. I take on a WC Fields mentality and urge them to take their little sticky fingers and chocolate covered complaining mouths away, far away. I make no apologies when it comes to fine chocolates.

For a chocolate lover, it's a real cocoa high of an event with chocolate sculptors, street artists, chocolate vendors, chocolate fondue stands and samples at every turn. In no time at all, I felt that familiar buzz, I felt dizzy, hands were sweating, my heart beating an all-out charge, my blood pressure inching up ever higher, my eyes felt as if they were going to pop out of my head. In other words, I was in choco-heaven, but it was a high which sadly would not last. Eventually I would sink down into a deep, never-ending abyss as my blood sugar desperately attempted to wrestle itself to normalcy. I dragged my sluggish body to the nearest cafe and collapsed in a chair and ordered twin IVs of water and coffee. Oh and *un pastis, deux glaçons s'il vous plaît.* Truly a memorable moment.

I resurfaced later that evening and decided that I would try *Le Café de la Place* on the advice of Mme. Chirpy herself. The restaurant/bistro was in *Vieux* Cannet so I could roll home if I had to. I found *Le Café* to be *un endroit très sympa* in other words a very friendly, welcoming *resto.* It is a well-kept secret but not for very long I suspect One of their marks of excellence is that they lean heavily on fresh local produce so if you're looking for Maryland crab cakes on the menu, you're going to be disappointed. I started with the *terrine de foie gras aux figues* and I have not had such delicious *foie gras* in a long-long time and told the owners just that. I then permitted myself to have the *pennes al dente au magret fumé* (smoked duck breast) and infused with black truffle. Good God! I pinched myself twice to make sure I was truly awake for this piece or was I heaven looking down. What an amazing dish and if you are a truffle hound as I am, I you will understand that it was almost better than something else. Thank goodness I had the sense God gave me to order a bottle of nicely chilled champagne *Veuve Clicquot Ponsardin* because truly, it paired beautifully. It was a perfect moment. It was my very own heaven on earth. As I was eating light, I decided to have their famous *Baba au Rhum* which is topped with a fine twelve-year-old Havana rum. *Salud!* I had coffee but passed on the little chocolates putting them in my pocket instead. Such willpower!

Seafood Risotto Dinner on the rue *Masséna* in Nice

A city like Nice has over a thousand places to eat, at least that's what I was told by my taxi driver as I was coming in from the airport. I think he may have been right, and I would say that at least half of them were located on the rue Masséna (named after André Masséna one of the original eighteen Marshals of the Empire created by Napoleon). There's a cocktail factoid that should make your admiring entourage hungry for more. If I may digress, cocktail factoids are an integral part of cocktail conversation. The trick is to use them carefully and strategically. Allow me to return to my most excellent discussion about the rue Massena. The rue is really a pedestrian walkway, and one naturally assumes it to be free of autos. My advice is to stay alert to that occasional hybrid/electric car slowly sneaking up behind you unnoticed followed by the horn. I speak from experience.

The Rue Masséna runs parallel to the beach and the famous *Promenade des Anglais* and it's lined with little shops, fancy boutiques on the rue Paradis (Vuitton, Chanel, and Cartier among others) and more than your share of outdoor cafes and crowded restaurants advertising everything from *prix fixe* menu to plain ol' pizza du pays. I was there once a few years back in November and all I can say is God help those who insist on coming down for the summer. I can guarantee one thing, you won't see me there unless I just happen to be in Cannes for the film festival and on the red carpet to accept my award for some valuable contribution to society. Might be interesting.

Le Milo's is your definition of a busy restaurant at 15 rue Masséna. Le Milo's, along with most of the other restaurants flirt dangerously on the edge of being a certified tourist trap with all the trimmings of being indifferent to the needs of those not speaking French or worse those attempting in vain to speak French. I realize that not all restaurants appeal to everyone just as not all restaurants deserve to be described as traps. If you are a tourist in Nice, you quickly realize you are not in Johnson City, Nagasaki, or London. So, my advice (once again) please act accordingly and behave responsibly. Le Milo has a varied menu with a lot of the traditional dishes but this time, I decided to go with the special of the day which happened to be a seafood risotto. I am glad I did as it was extremely tasty, and it arrived table-side with a selection of calamari, mussels, and clams over a steaming bed of creamy risotto. On top of it all was a super-sized prawn who was clearly in charge of the dish. With the help of a bottle of dry white wine from Provence, I made my way through this most excellent dish. Desert as always is a challenge with so much to choose from. I decided on simplicity with a crepe and vanilla ice cream and concluded with a Cognac, just to be polite.

HORS-SEASON – ANTIBES/ JUAN LES PINS

There is this wonderful song by the French singer, *Francis Cabrel*, who is from the south of France, appropriately called "*Hors-season*" or "Off-season." Allow me to pen the first few lines of this song that I find very evocative: "It's the silence That's most noticeable. The rolling blinds all down. Old weeds in the flowerpots on the balconies. It must be off-season."

I am sure there are those of you who have spent some time at seasonal resorts when the tourists have all gone home, school has started, little shops close down with a solemn promise that they will return next year. I love the off-season, but I will admit it can get a little sad and even, yes, a bit melancholy. I will also admit that I find there is a sense of charm in these little towns absent the mad rush of tourists. I remember when I was returning to Brittany, usually around September – October time frame, I would drive through the little coastal towns where most of the homes overlooking the beach would be shut for the winter and, as the song writer *Cabrel* states, what's most noticeable are that the rolling blinds are all the way down and yes, a few forgotten flowerpots remain sitting in the corner waiting next spring.

I decided to spend five days in Antibes – Juan les Pins a delightful little seaside town that's whisper quiet during the off season, but I am told that things come dramatically alive in the summer when the beautiful people flock to town, expensive sporty little cars zip through the narrow little streets, the Jazz Festival kicks in, and hedonism comfortably settles in for the summer. But for me, I came in November certainly not for the bright lights and pulsating sounds emanating from dance clubs along the beach and certainly not to rub sun-tan lotion bodies with the beach goers and last but not least, I certainly did not come to bake under the relentless burning Mediterranean summer sun. I do not want to mislead the reader into thinking that the November days in Juan les Pins were something akin to a nuclear winter. Not by any means. In fact, yours truly grabbed a primo spot outside the *Café de la Plage* so that I too could join the sun worshippers during the few hours of the day when sun was nice and warm. There I was, nursing a *petit café*, and enjoying the idle chatter about me. A mix of languages, French du Midi as well as the occasional hints of Spanish, British, Eastern Europeans and perhaps Russian or other Eastern European language that I am not familiar with. Those restaurants, many lining the waterfront, are not all open in the off-season; some stay open if it's nice and warm during the day and will serve lunch while others open their door only in the evening. It's a comfortable pace and locals will readily admit the rhythm of life during the off season takes on a welcome but different beat. To be quite honest, I'm fine with that.

Just off the *Boulevard Edouard Baudoin*, is the Hotel Belles Rives once known as the "Villa Saint-Louis" and for a short time the home of F. Scoot Fitzgerald and his wife Zelda. I can so understand how this famous couple could have headed off for the French Riviera in 1925 and easily succumbed, as they did, to the charms of the "Villa" in a cozy cove on the Cap d' Antibes overlooking the beautiful Mediterranean Sea. It is here that Fitzgerald wrote his masterpiece, 'Tender is The Night' while Zelda most likely struggled with her own demons. They transformed the Villa Saint Louis into a fashionable resort home for wealthy Americans who were discovering the pleasures of wild partying, swimming in the sea then more wild partying. One can sit out on the patio, as I did, one morning for breakfast, enjoying the sun and was easily transported back to another era and could well imagine the elegance, and yes, the decadence, of the times and as Fitzgerald noted, those

"Special transitory moments when everything…seemed to be going well."

I think we have all had those moments at one time or another. I know I have. Someone noted appropriately that those days in the roaring '20s in the South of France were "indeed a life lived at night, with Champagne, extravagance, and sweet decadence." Sign me up and take me back those days, please I must insist! While not an abundance of restaurants that were open for lunch or dinner, there were more to choose from during the day and I took every opportunity to explore as many as my wallet could afford without protesting. One would stroll along the boardwalk with the Mediterranean Sea on one side and the many little shops, narrow street and the occasional condominiums on the right as one left Juan les Pins and blended into the town of Antibes.

There on the beach, I found a little seaside restaurant doing a thriving business; it called out my name and I could not resist.

Seated at a little table that was well dug into the sand, I enjoyed the gentle offshore breeze and took in the moment for all that it was worth. The big question *"du moment"* of course was red, white, or rose? A bottle of Rose de Provence won hands down! I perused the little menu more for fun and idle curiosity because I already knew what I wanted. *Moules et pomme* frites thank you very much and the wine nicely chilled please. There were, of course, the obligatory one or two little dogs lying quietly by their master's leg waiting for that little something to drop by accident or on purpose. It was a wonderful meal and a memorable moment by the sea. I did not want it to ever end, let alone have to leave this side of paradise.

Back to the Wine Futures

This is a story about a much-anticipated 2009 vine vintage. In retrospect, for much of the wine world, this vintage was indeed excellent.

Something very important is being whispered about from person to person in alleyways, side streets, over cups of strong sweet coffee at the *Ortakoy Princell* Hotel in Istanbul; in lofts between the sheets (of course); in the Eiffel Tower elevators; over lunch at Chez Marcel in the Marais district; in Mayfair it's mentioned rather matter-of-factly by one's tailor on Savile Row; at a private club over a fine malt scotch with only a splash of soda and the Financial Times; by Emile your doorman along with a wink and a nod of approval; by that lady at 53rd and Madison, the one with two yappy poodles; or overheard above the persistent techno beat at the "Propaganda" on *Bolshoi Zlatustinsky* 7 in Moscow. War be damned. But what is going on?? What's being whispered? Simply put it's all about "2009." Was that a code signaling troop movements in Ukraine? Was it then, perhaps, a long-lost Panzer division spotted crossing the border into France? Or was it a code that, when matched to the Cyrillic alphabet would reveal a cunning spy operation? Maybe it just stood for a newer version of Windows (please no!)

The 2009 whispering frenzy was all about a most anticipated banner year for French Bordeaux's. Some well-placed wags who must drink a lot, decreed that it would surely surpass 2005 and in fact would go down as being the best in living memory, thanks to last year's perfect conditions of a wet spring and hot summer. Growers, a temperamental and suspicious lot in the best of times, are becoming increasingly convinced that 2009 may be as good as the near-perfect 2005 vintage-if not better; the mix of nice warm days but cool, dry nights in the final days before grape picking began was the finest since 1949. That's stepping out on a limb. I tried remembering what the wine was like in 1949 and did not have any luck. My parents were in Paris, but I had yet to make my appearance. Apparently, the cool nights stopped the grapes from over-ripening and added sophistication. July and August were ideally hot and sunny. Then just when drought threatened to stop the grapes from ripening and developing crucial tannins to help age the wines, the rain came. It all sounded almost poetic.

My friends the Chinese, who have replaced tea with a good Bordeaux as their national drink of choice are not ones to sit idly about when there is money to be made off so many Capitalist running dogs; they were already trying to corner the market on the '09 vintage and with some limited success. Let a million vineyards grow, that's my motto. But I am philosophical, carefully pragmatic and one who looks toward the future, any good future in fact.

The rush from Asia can only lead to driving up the prices on these beauties. I see a time when there will be little flags fluttering all across the People's Provinces of France. There ought to be a Congressional panel looking into this – whatever "this" really is. I am just thinking that it would be awfully nice to see Congress finally wake-up and do something meaningful about an issue that I really care about, that would be good red wine, rather than wasting their time developing meaningless political soundbites for gullible public consumption

Let me return to the point I believe I was trying to make but which may have gotten lost in translation. Playing the futures game is a reasonable approach to obtaining decently priced early wines now and bet on improving your investment sometime in the future. The upside, say as an example you order a case of 2009 *Saint-Emilion* at a per bottle price of US $14.00. At this point, it is still maturing in the barrels and has not yet been bottled. For argument's sake, in 2012, the third year after the vintage, you receive a call (not a margin call – those you run from) that the 2012's have made their appearance and please come and pick up you "stash." With a little research you see that your wine is now selling for US $22.50, nice. You can drink it now if you must or you can place it in your cellar for another five years at which time you will be enjoying a nice and far more expensive vintage. Or wait to give it to your children in the sure and certain knowledge they will be having one heck of a party and thanking the old man. Downside to all of this, you get your wine, you decide to hold on to it and it turns out to be, well not as grandiose as what some of the experts were touting. Still not a bad deal. There you go a crash course in wino economics 101. Whine all you want but I encourage you to investigate. Listen to the whisper!

SWORDFISH NIÇOISE; *ESPADON À LA NIÇOISE*

"Then the fish came alive, with his death in him, and rose high out of the water showing all his great length and width and all his power and his beauty. He seemed to hang in the air above the old man in the skiff. Then he fell into the water with a crash that sent spray over the old man and over all of the skiff."
Ernest Hemingway – The Old Man and the Sea

My good friend Luc made my mission as clear as possible. Go to Beaulieu-sur-Mer and he would meet up with me and then we would go fishing. I asked him where would he be? Sometimes I ask the wrong questions. I was off, a man on a mission.

I half expected *Beaulieu-sur-Mer* to be a sleepy little town with a slow and comfortable *vas-et-vient* pace to it, with fishing nets everywhere, boat hulls being lazily repainted in vibrant colors under the hot Mediterranean sun, perhaps a few crusty locals sipping on a *pastis* outside "*Chez Marcel*" your run-of-the-mill honky-tonk bar with, most likely, an anchor hanging over the front door. Inside, someone was slowly sweeping the past evening's events into a corner and Marcel, the owner, wiping and re-wiping the shiny zinc countertop. There would surely be a requisite rummy or two in striped *matelots* shirts working on their first jolt of the day, maybe even a frosted blond busting out of a dress a few sizes too small and weighing her morning odds with the two rummy's. But clearly it was I who was delusional and suffering from too much time in the hot sun.

Crossing the *Boulevard du Maréchal Joffre*, I dodged a few high-end Mercedes, and I almost knocked over a couple who were perfectly tanned and impeccably dressed and busily scanning their smart phones undoubtedly for *une bonne addresse* where they could see and be seen and all the while conversing in a mixture of French and Italian. Tanned statuesque beauties were out walking their little specimen dogs, two by two as if on parade. I strolled along stopping every so often to look over menu boards in front of interesting looking restaurants then quickly realizing my bank account would not even get me past the appetizers. I could smell money, it hovered everywhere. A light tap on my shoulder, I turned to find Luc who asked, "are we fishing today or are you going to waste my time mixing with the beautiful people?" I never did learn how Luc found me.

Part IV

SELECTED RECIPES

I have put forth some great dishes for you to consider. I have cooked them all at one time or another, and to be frank, some may have come out more spectacular than others. So what? Half the fun in French cooking is first uncorking a good wine, turning on a little music, Edith Piaf or Charles Aznavour perhaps, then getting those frying pans rocking 'n rolling. You can do it! The only person stopping you is yourself. If I can tackle these dishes, then I know you can. Remember, you just can't go wrong with ingredients such as cream, Cognac, Calvados, mustard, plenty of butter, and even more wine. Final word of advice, be not afraid to improvise. Fortune favors the bold.

<u>Roasted Chicken with Lemon and Rosemary</u>

This roasted chicken takes a little preparation and also a little patience. You are on vacation so no worries. Browning the chicken before roasting can get a little messy. The small hassle is time well spent, though; the flavor is superior to that of more simply prepared roasts. Just think of the big smiles on little Gaston and Arlette when they see this dish. If Monsieur is doing the cooking, Madame will have that special smile for you....*c'est compris*? Madame if you are the cook ask Monsieur to take off his beret, à table, and possibly put on a shirt.

Total Time: 1 hour, 45 minutes

Ingredients:

(Gentle reminder, this is for 8 so if cooking for two please adjust unless you really like chicken!)

1/2 cup plus 4 tablespoons extra virgin olive oil, divided

16 pearl onions, peeled and trimmed (most summer markets will have these for sure)

5 carrots, peeled and cut into 2-inch pieces

4 celery stalks, cut into 2-inch pieces

4 cloves of garlic, separated and peeled

1 3/4 teaspoon salt, divided

3/4 teaspoon ground black pepper, divided

1 (4-5 lb.) chicken, rinsed and patted dry

1 lemon (peeled, pitted and sliced)

1 tablespoon plus 2 teaspoons lemon zest
1 tablespoon fresh parsley, chopped
1 tablespoon fresh rosemary, chopped
1/2 teaspoon dried thyme
1/3 cup Chardonnay or your regular white wine *"vin maison"*
1 cup chicken stock

Preparation:

Preheat oven to 450F. Heat 2 tablespoons of the olive oil in a large, heavy skillet over medium-high heat. Add the onions, carrots, celery, garlic cloves, ¾ teaspoon salt, and ¼ teaspoon pepper, and cook, stirring occasionally, for 10 minutes. When the vegetables are caramelized, spoon them along the sides of a large roasting pan and set it aside.

Reduce the burner heat slightly and allow the pan to cool a bit. Add 2 tablespoons oil to pan and return the pan to medium-high heat. Season the prepared chicken with the remaining salt and pepper, and brown it in the hot oil. Transfer the chicken to the center of the roasting pan, carefully cut 1-inch slits into the skin, and pour the pan juices on top of the chicken. Very carefully pull open the slits in the skin and rub the lemon zest, parsley, rosemary, and thyme under the skin. Put the lemon slices, additional Rosemary and 4 cloves of garlic in the chicken.

Add the wine to the skillet and deglaze, scraping up any browned bits from the pan. After the wine has simmered for 30 seconds, add the chicken stock and heat through. Pour the wine sauce over the chicken. Cover the roasting pan with a lid or tightly sealed foil and roast in the preheated oven for 60-70 minutes, until the chicken tests 170 when a thermometer is inserted in the thigh. You may wish to broil the chicken for about 10 minutes after taking off the foil just to give it a nice brown color. Allow the chicken to stand at room temperature in the pan for 10 minutes before carving.

Serves 8.

Serving Suggestions: Toss green salad vinaigrette, local cheese, fresh baguette from your new Boulangerie and potatoes and parsley.

Now about wines... Well, you are on vacation, right? So, you have to live off the land therefore maybe something like a nice Rose or a New Zealand Sauvignon Blanc (delicious!) or even a dry Riesling. Yes, I will go out on a broad reach here and there. Oh, and be a nice fellow and invite your neighbors unless there's a good reason not to do so.

Chicken with Onions, Calvados, and Cream
(*Poussin Vallée d'Auge*)

I have to add that this has been a real crowd pleaser and you know it when they start licking their plates. Yes, it's a little bit more involved to bring it all together but it is a delicious recipe. There are just too many things to love in this recipe. It happens.

There are two ways that one can prepare this dish. One way is in a large pan (some would argue, perhaps the more traditional style) or second, cooked slowly in an oven. Either way is fine or believe me, the end result is equally delicious. *Poussins* are 1-lb. squab chickens, larger and meatier than Cornish game hens. This classic Norman preparation, named for the superior Calvados-producing region of Pays d'Auge, can be adapted to larger chickens, an ex, other fowl, or pork. In this instance and to remain true to the recipe, I will leave it as our six cute little *poussins* who lost their way home.

Ingredients

6 cute little poussins (or 2 boneless chicken breasts filet per serving)
2 small apples (tart variety)
Salt and freshly ground black pepper
4 tbsp. softened butter
3 1/2 oz chicken stock or fresh cider (from the press out back)
1 cup of button mushrooms (or champignon de Paris)
2 cups pearl onions
1/2 cup+ calvados (I suppose you could use ordinary brandy, just don't tell me)
3/4 cup heavy cream or creme fraiche (ideal)

Directions

Preheat oven to 400°. Wash the birds thoroughly, then drain and dry with paper towels. Rub them with salt inside and out. Pepper each one generously.

Truss poussins in this manner: Fold wing tips back beneath shoulders. Drumsticks should fit snugly against the tips of breastbone. Hold in place by tying the legs together with kitchen twine, then wrap long pieces of twine around the birds to hold things close to body, then wrap it back around the birds and close up tail pieces. Tie twine in bows so it's easy to untie after cooking.

Rub birds with butter. Arrange in an oven-proof pan so they do not touch. Scatter peeled onions around birds.

Quarter and core apples and cut into small cubes, add-in half the apples and the mushrooms.

Place pan in lower third of oven and cook for at least 45 minutes, basting several times. Prick fat part of drumstick on 1 bird after 45 minutes. If juice runs clear and drumstick moves easily in its socket, birds are done.

Transfer the now compliant *poussins* and onions to a serving platter. Scrape pan drippings into a saucepan with a rubber spatula, bring to a boil, reduce heat, and simmer for 2 minutes. Use chicken stock as necessary. Add in remaining half of apples. Warm Calvados (take a shot just to be sure), add to the pan juices, and flame. When flames die out and you've collected your eyebrows, stir in cream, and continue to reduce sauce until thickened. Adjust seasonings as needed with salt and pepper. Pour sauce over and around poussins and serve.

Serves 6

Serving suggestions

Lightly fry off large slices of French bread (one per portion) to make a crouton and lay this on a large, warmed plate. Place chicken on the crouton and mask with the cream sauce. Garnish with a sliced apple and a little parsley and serve to your famished guests!

Now about wines...

Chinon from the Val de Loire. My goodness this is an incredibly easy wine to love if you like Beaujolais. Great dinner companion.

You may also like a Vouvray which just happens to be one of my daughter's favorites, and I can see why.

<u>Pan-Fried Steaks with Mustard Cream Sauce</u>

This is a real crowd-pleaser and it's easy to put together. I mean anything with mustard, cream, and cognac, how could anything go wrong or not taste delicious?

This is bistro cuisine at its finest. I tip my chef's hat to that cozy restaurant *Chez George* on the Rue du Mail in Paris (*un véritable bistrot bourgeois parisien*), comes this classic and ever popular dish. Some years ago, the Figaro listed this popular dish from *Chez George* as one of 10 *plats addictifs* or ten most addictive meals (the French do not good food lightly.) I doubt if they have changed their minds since then. This particular recipe includes some of my all-time favorite ingredients: mustard, cream, cognac and of course a meal that could only be served up with heaping *pommes allumettes,* a green salad and all pleasantly washed down with a good bottle of *Chinon* from the Loire Valley. If I may be so bold as to suggest, please indulge yourself in having a *Baba au Rhum* for dessert. It's a little peek into heaven, I assure you! It arrives completely saturated with rum (always a good start) and filled with whipped cream or pastry cream.

In the end, this meal is a recipe for your own true happiness, forget the guests. This is all about you and your God-given right to be satisfied. Truly a wonderful moment indeed. You can worry about redemption later! This recipe is adapted from *Saveur* Magazine and based in part on Daniel Young's *The Bistros, Brasseries, and Wine Bars of Paris*. I have tweaked it here and there. The squeals of delight are, of course, all yours.

Ingredients:

4 8–10-oz. flat iron steaks, cut horizontally without the connective tissue
Kosher salt and freshly ground black pepper, to taste
1 tbsp. unsalted butter
1 tbsp. canola oil
5 tbsp. cognac or brandy
1/4 cup heavy cream
1 1/2 tbsp. Dijon mustard
1 tbsp. minced flat-leaf parsley

Directions:

Season flat iron steaks with salt and pepper. Heat butter and oil in a 12" cast-iron skillet over medium-high heat. The term "flat iron" is sometimes referred to as a "top blade" roast. In the UK, they call it a Butler's steak. I wonder about that.

Add steaks and cook, turning once, until browned and cooked to desired temperature, about 6 minutes for medium rare. Remove pan from heat. Transfer steaks to 4 warm plates and pour off and discard all but 1 tbsp. fat.

Add 4 1⁄2 tbsp. cognac to pan and stir, scraping browned bits from the bottom with a wooden spoon. Return pan to medium-high heat and cook for 20 seconds.

Add cream and mustard, season with salt and pepper, and cook, stirring vigorously, until sauce just comes together. Stir in remaining cognac and pour sauce over steaks.

Serve steaks garnished with parsley and black pepper.

Now, about wine…

If a Chinon is not your style, a California Lioco Indica Mendocino Red Wine has a smoky berry flavor that offsets the richness of the steak and I find it very appealing.

Serves 4

<u>Rabbit in Mustard Sauce</u>

This recipe (modified by yours truly, of course because I can) comes from David Tanis, a chef at Chez Panisse in Berkeley, California. This dish was inspired by the rabbit stew our dear cook would lovingly put together in Brittany. The rabbit never stood a chance.

Ingredients:

I will spare the reader the sordid details about the rabbit's pre-preparation. Those sordid details are perhaps best left in the kitchen away from the delicate eyes and ears of family and guests.

2 unlucky rabbits (about 2 1⁄2 lbs. each),each cut into 6–8 pieces or a hare more if you wish.

Kosher salt and freshly ground black pepper, to taste

1/2 lb. pancetta or unsmoked bacon, cut into 1/4"-thick strips

1 cup of sliced mushrooms

1 1/2 cups *crème fraîche* **Note: If you do not have any CF use 1/2 cup each of sour cream and whipping cream (for 1 cup) and let stand for 12 hours; or use Mascarpone cheese as an alternative. Or just a glass of wine for contemplation purposes. (I have often chosen the last alternative.)

1 cup Dijon mustard

1 – 2 cups white wine

2 tbsp. roughly chopped fresh thyme

2 tbsp. roughly chopped fresh sage

2 tsp. black or yellow mustard seeds, crushed

8 garlic cloves, thinly sliced

4 bay leaves

Directions:

1. Season rabbit generously with salt and pepper and place in a large bowl along with remaining ingredients. Don't go stingy on the mustard as some of its flavor will get lost in cooking.

2. Mix together with your hands until rabbit pieces are coated. Cover bowl with plastic wrap and let marinate at room temperature for at least 1 hour or overnight in the refrigerator. Yes, you have to wait.

3. If rabbit has been chilled, allow it to come to room temperature. Heat oven to 400° and arrange a rack in the middle of your oven.

4. Divide rabbit in a single layer between 2 shallow roasting pans and top with any of the remaining marinade.
5. Roast the rabbit, add the wine, turning rabbit once and basting with pan juices occasionally, until the juices have reduced and rabbit is cooked through, about 55 minutes.
6. With 15 minutes left to go on the cooking, add the mushrooms. Important: Pour yourself another glass of wine.
7. Set oven to broil and cook until golden brown, about 5 minutes more. Serve rabbit with pan juices.

Serves 6-8

Serving suggestions:
Add 8 small red potatoes, quartered, to the dish mid-way through the cooking cycle, that way they will absorb all the delicious juices. Finger-lickin' good *mes amis*.

Now about wines…
Chinon, Val de Loire
Coteaux du Languedoc

<u>Seared Scallops with Tarragon-Butter Sauce</u>
(Thank you Gourmet Magazine)

"Benjamin, I have just two words for you….are you listening carefully Benjamin? Beurre Blanc." (Apologies to *The Graduate*)

Classic French butter sauce easy to prepare and let's face it, tends to make just about anything taste better. In this recipe, *Beurre Blanc* uses the scallops' juices to add complexity. There are so many variations on scallop recipes so feel free to adjust as you like and call it yours.

Ingredients:

1 1/4 pounds large sea scallops (oddly enough), tough ligament from side of each discarded
7 tablespoons unsalted butter, cut into tablespoons, divided
2 tablespoons finely chopped shallot
1/4 cup dry white wine
1/4 cup white-wine vinegar
Sea salt and freshly ground black pepper
1 tablespoon finely chopped tarragon

Directions:

Pat scallops dry and sprinkle with 1/4 teaspoon each of salt and pepper (total).

Heat 1 tablespoon butter in a 12-inch non-stick skillet over medium-high heat until foam subsides, then sear the scallops, turning once, until golden brown and just cooked through, about 5 minutes total.

Transfer to a platter.

Add shallot, wine, and vinegar to skillet and boil, scraping up brown bits, until reduced to 2 tablespoons.

Add juices from platter and if necessary boil until liquid is reduced to about 1/4 cup.

Reduce heat to low and add 3 tablespoons butter, stirring until almost melted, then add remaining 3 tablespoons butter and swirl until incorporated and sauce has a creamy consistency.

Stir in tarragon and salt to taste; pour sauce over scallops.

Serve will new potatoes, green salad, and baguette.
Serves 4

Now about wine…
Loire Valley, *Muscadet – Sèvre et Maine sur Lie.*

<u>Poulet à la Normande</u>
Adapted from NYT Cooking

Let me state that this dish may seem a bit more daunting than you might otherwise wish (Nonsense, as my father would often say) rest assured, work through the dish methodically, have a glass of wine or two, and it will all come together. You won't be sorry you did. There are any number of variations on this dish but as always, I have tried to add my touch where I thought it was needed. Alternatively, you can just order a pizza.

Ingredients:
1 (3 1/2-pound) chicken, cut into 8 bone-in pieces
Salt and freshly ground black pepper
5 tablespoons butter
2 tablespoons olive oil
2 onions, diced

2 carrots, diced

3 sprigs thyme

1 bay leaf

1/2 cup *Calvados*

1 cup apple cider *(cidre brut, svp)*

1 cup chicken stock

30 pearl onions

3 medium apples, peeled, cored and cut into 8 wedges *(the ones in your orchard should be fine)* & 1 cup *crème fraîche.*

Directions:

Season the chicken with salt and pepper. In a large, heavy saucepan, melt 2 tablespoons of the butter with the olive oil over medium-high heat. Add the chicken skin-side down and brown on all sides. Transfer to a plate.

Pour off most of the fat from the pan. Add the onions, carrots, thyme, and bay leaf and cook until the onions are translucent, about 5 minutes. Add the *Calvados*, warm slightly, then stand back and ignite it. Once the flames die, and you still have some hair on your head, add the cider, scraping up the brown bits. Bring to a boil and reduce by half. Add the stock and return the chicken to the pan. Simmer, covered, for 20 minutes. Transfer the breast pieces to a bowl. Cook the legs and thighs for 10 more minutes and add to the bowl. Keep warm.

Meanwhile, soak the pearl onions in warm water before peeling. Melt 2 tablespoons butter in a large skillet. Add the onions and a pinch of salt, cover, and cook over medium heat for 10 minutes, shaking the pan occasionally. Uncover, add 1 tablespoon butter, and increase heat to medium-high. Place the apples in the center of the pan. Sear on each side for 10 to 15 minutes, until caramelized.

Strain the *Calvados* sauce and return it to the pan. Add the juices from the chicken. Whisk in the *crème fraîche*. Simmer until the sauce coats the back of a spoon. Season. Add the chicken pieces and warm through

Serving Suggestions: Serve with *sautéed* mushrooms and *sautéed* potatoes, or green peas and braised onions. I'm starved!! Perhaps a little *Calva* to get us all going?

Serves 4

Now about wine…

Côtes du Roussillon, 2007 Blanc "Les Pierres Plates"

<u>Gratineed Chicken in Cream Sauce</u>
Poulet à la Fermière

This is a wonderful dish, and it brings back the delicious home cooking I so enjoyed in Brittany.

Ingredients:

2 pounds chicken thighs and drumsticks *(I used all thighs)*1 tablespoon unsalted butter

6 fresh parsley sprigs

2 fresh thyme sprigs

1 bay leaf

4 carrots, cut diagonally into 1-inch-thick slices

2 cups frozen (or pearl) small whole onions, thawed and patted dry

1/2 cup dry white wine

1/3 cup chicken broth
1 pound small (1 1/2-inch) boiling potatoes, peeled and halved
2/3 cup *crème fraîche*
1 cup frozen baby peas, thawed
1 cup coarsely grated *Gruyère*

Special equipment: a small square of cheesecloth and a willing chicken.

Directions:

Pat chicken dry and season with salt and pepper.

Heat butter in a 12-inch oven-proof deep heavy *sauté* pan over moderately high heat until foam subsides, then brown chicken all over, in batches, if necessary, 8 to 10 minutes. Transfer to a plate and cover. Pour off all but 1 tablespoon fat from pan.

Tie parsley, thyme, and bay leaf in cheesecloth to make a bouquet garni, then add to pan with carrots and onions, stirring to coat with fat. Add wine and deglaze by boiling over high heat, stirring, and scraping up brown bits, until liquid is reduced by half, about 3 minutes. Add broth and chicken, skin sides up, with any juices from plate, and simmer, covered, 10 minutes. Add potatoes and salt and pepper to taste and simmer, covered, until chicken is cooked through, and potatoes are tender, about 15 minutes.

Preheat broiler.

Discard bouquet garni. Stir in *crème fraiche*, peas, and salt and pepper to taste, then turn chicken in sauce to coat. Sprinkle dish all over with *Gruyère* and broil 4 to 5 inches from heat until browned and sauce is bubbling, 3 to 4 minutes.
Serves 4

Serve with a tossed green salad and a crusty baguette to help you wipe your plate clean.

Now about wine…
Nicolas Joly "*Coulée de Serrant*" Loire Valley

Swordfish Niçoise / *Espadon À La Niçoise*

A touch of Nice is beautiful! You will be making plans to fly south before you know it!

Ingredients:
4 swordfish steaks (about 6 ounces each)
1 large clove of garlic
Coarse salt, to taste
2 1/2 tablespoons red-wine vinegar
1/3 cup plus 2 tablespoons extra-virgin olive oil
Freshly ground black pepper, to taste
4 red new potatoes
8 ounces tender green beans, ends snapped, halved diagonally and blanched
1/2 cup diced (1/4 inch) red bell pepper
1/2 small red onion, slivered lengthwise

1/4 cup pitted Niçoise olives

1 tablespoon drained tiny capers

1/4 cup loosely packed slivered basil leaves

2 tablespoons fresh lemon juice

1 hard-cooked egg, coarsely chopped

1 teaspoon rosemary

2 tablespoons chopped flat-leaf parsley

Directions:

Throw three or four fishing poles into your skiff and head out to sea well past the other fishermen to your own fishing spot and drop your lines; as the sun rises slowly take a careful, measured sip of water and wait for one of your lines to tug suddenly and hard...game on!

1. Add salt and a generous portion of garlic; mince and place in a large shallow bowl with the vinegar. Slowly drizzle in 1/3 cup olive oil, whisking constantly to make a vinaigrette. Season with pepper.

2. Cook the potatoes in boiling salted water until tender but not mushy, about 10 minutes. Drain. Slice the potatoes and place in a bowl. Layer the green beans atop the potatoes, followed by the red pepper, onion, olives, capers, and slivered fresh basil. Do not toss this salad until serving time.

3. Preheat the broiler. Meanwhile, combine the remaining 2 tablespoons olive oil, lemon juice, salt, and pepper in a bowl. Add the fish, coat well. Let rest 15 minutes.

4. Place the fish on a lightly oiled broiler pan, 4 inches from the heat source, and broil for 4 minutes on the first side. Turn carefully and broil 4 minutes on the other side. Remove to the center of a platter.

5. Gently toss the salad from underneath and surround the swordfish. Sprinkle the chopped egg on top. Grind some pepper and garnish with chopped parsley.

Serves 4

Now about a wine…
Puligny-Montrachet Joseph Drouhin

Fricassée of Chicken with Vouvray Wine
Fricassée de Volaille au Vouvray

(Adapted from a recipe by *Chef Francois Salle* when he was at the *Auberge de la Brenne. Thank you.*) I must add that this is a stunningly delicious dish. Please, take me back to the Loire Valley!

Ingredients:
1 large free-range chicken, about 4 lbs.
2 bouquet *garnis*: 2 bay leaves, 2 thyme sprigs, 12 parsley sprigs
2 carrots, halved
1 onion, quartered
3 tablespoons unsalted butter
2 tablespoons all-purpose flour
1 1/2 cups (12 oz) dry Vouvray

salt and freshly cracked pepper
3 oz. white mushrooms
pinch of chervil
pinch of chopped tarragon
Chicken stock *(see option 2)*
1 egg yolk
2 tablespoons of *crème fraiche* or heavy (double) cream

Preparation

First open a bottle of Vouvray and pour a glass just to make sure it meets your expectations.

Then cut the chicken into serving pieces

Option 1 (traditional) place the carcass, neck, gizzard, and heart in a large saucepan with 1 bouquet *garni,* the carrots and onions. Add cold water to cover dem' bones and vegetables. Bring to boil and simmer for 30 minutes. Option 2 (I'm in a hurry and desperate mood) discard the carcass and reach for a quart of chicken broth. Option 3 (and you did not hear this from me) Buy a chicken that has already been cut up. It will save time.

Melt the butter in a casserole. Add the chicken pieces and sauté over medium-high heat until lightly browned on all sides (5+ minutes per side).

Sprinkle the flour evenly over the chicken pieces. Add the Vouvray (taste again to ensure consistent quality control) and add the remaining bouquet *garni.*

When the stock has simmered pour it through one real fine strainer and add enough of it to the chicken to cover it by about 1 inch. Season with salt and pepper and simmer, covered, over low heat for 35 minutes.

Remove 4 cups of the cooking liquid from the chicken and place it in a saucepan with the mushrooms, chervil and tarragon and simmer briskly.

Combine the egg yolk and the *crème fraiche* and whisk it into the mushroom mixture without allowing the sauce to boil.

Arrange the chicken pieces on a warmed serving platter. Spoon the sauce evenly over the chicken and sprinkle with chopped parsley, if desired. Serve with steamed potatoes. I would expect a plate cheeses of course, and some fruit -maybe for desert...or maybe not.

Serves 4-6

Now about wine...
Domaine Vigneau-Chevreau Vouvray Cuvée Silex**,** *Loire, France*

<u>Sautéed Pork Chops in Green Peppercorn Mustard Cream Sauce</u>

I found this little recipe and was wonderfully intrigued, not having worked with green peppercorn mustard before. It sounded so good that I sat down at the kitchen table and with a full glass of *Jean-Marc Burgaud Morgon Vieilles Vignes* at arm's reach (never further,) and studied this gem more carefully. After thinking this over, I concluded that another glass of wine was needed. I then reached a verdict. Get thee to a kitchen and make this dish. *Et voila* ladies and gentlemen a wonderful little dish to be enjoyed by family and friends alike. You know, maybe what attracted me in the first place was that it reminded me of a little bistro in Paris, in 16e arrondissement I used to frequent quite often with one amie or another. *Madame la patronne,* would greet me with open arms *"mon petit Americain"* and would usher me *à table* and in the process, telling me what I was having for dinner. I just know this selection is something she would have urged me to try without even letting me read the menu. I like that.

<u>Pork Chops in a Green Peppercorn Mustard Sauce</u>
Cotes de Porc a la creme de Moutarde au
Poivre Vert
(Adapted in part from Good Life Family
magazine)

Ingredients:
4 nice size pork chops
Flour
1 tbsp of olive oil
1 oz of butter
2 large shallots
1 glass of dry white wine
4 tbsp. of *crème fraiche*
1 egg yoke
1 tsp of lemon juice
2 tbsp of green peppercorn mustard
Salt and pepper

Directions:

Salt and pepper and add a dusting of flour on each side of the chops then brown them in a pan with the oil and melted butter.

Once the chops are nicely brown on each side add in the chopped shallots and the white wine. Bring to a boil then cover and cook at medium temperature for 15 minutes. Test the white wine to ensure its integrity.

Once the chops are cooked, set them aside on a warm plate or pop them in a heated over. Don't dry them out, please.

Return the pan to the heat and scrape the bottom with a wooden spoon to get all those delicious bits waiting for you. Add in the *crème fraîche* letting it thicken all the while stirring like a mad man.

In a little bowl, gently beat the egg yolk adding the lemon juice and mustard. Incorporate the ingredients, thoroughly mixed, into the warm *crème,* bit by bit. Check the seasoning and add as needed. Add a spoonful of the sauce on top of each chop, place on a platter with the rest of the sauce.

Serving suggestions: I would present this with new red potatoes on the side, a basket of crusty baguette slices and a *pichet vin maison.* Alternatively, spoil yourself with plateful of frites.
　Serves4

Now about wine...

2010 Jean-Marc Burgaud Beaujolais-Village "Les Vignes de Thulon." Delicious.

<u>Thon à la Basquaise</u> (Tuna Basque-style)

Easy to put together and incredibly delicious!
You will want to wear your beret for this one.

Ingredients:

6 slices of tuna

4 tomatoes

4 onions

3 green peppers

4 cloves of garlic

1 *bouquet garni* (parsley, thyme, and bay leaf)

2 sprigs of parsley

6 oz fish stock

6 oz dry white wine

3 oz olive oil

sea salt and cracked black pepper

Cooking Instructions:

Slice onions and chop the garlic. Wash the green peppers remove the seeds, cut in two then again into slices. Dice the tomatoes.

Heat the oil in a large pan then you cook the onions, garlic, peppers and tomatoes for 2 minutes. Add salt and pepper.

Lower the heat then add half the white wine having tasted it first. Add the *bouquet garni* then cover and cook at very low heat for about an hour.

Meanwhile, chop the parsley then add the remaining white wine and stock and bring to a boil.

Introduce your tuna slices to the frying pan and cook for about 10 minutes.

Place the tuna slices on a platter and spoon the *sauce basquaise*, sprinkle with parsley and serve immediately to your hungry guests. Serve with rice and a smile.

Serves 6

Now about wine…
Château Malartic-Lagravière Blanc: A very fresh and appealing wine, clean and bright. A wonderful dinner companion, I might add.

ABOUT THE AUTHOR

The author at the family house in Brittany

Richard H. Rogers is a third-generation francophone. His paternal grandmother arrived in Paris as a young woman in 1913 for the last social season before the Great War; his father grew up in Paris in the 1920's and later returned during the war and later after the war. The author's early Paris years were in the 1950's and 1960's. France, its people, culture, and way of life and most importantly food are all inextricably encoded in his DNA. He has two lovely grown children and three beautiful grandchildren.

He writes about those themes he is most deeply passionate about: his experiences in France as young boy in Paris or in the idyllic French countryside. As an adult, he loves putting together a great story with an even greater meal. The family home, along the rugged Brittany coastline, remains a never-ending source of inspiration and deep sentimentality for much of his writing.

His inspiration to begin writing was a "pounding need" in him to recount his years growing up Paris and surviving his French school years and also the long, idyllic summers spent in Brittany, a part of France that he deeply treasures to this day and the memories have been burned in him. The author has travelled the globe extensively that he writes about his travel adventures, what he sees and also the food he eats. Translating the visual richness of other cultures, China, Vietnam, Turkey, India or anywhere else into meaningful short stories remains an exciting and enduring challenge.

He owes his love and deep appreciation for French food to two women in his life: his mother who was an excellent cook in her own right and daily would prepare incredible meals; and, in Brittany to Simone, the loving, family cook, who was, in reality, so much more than that. He grew up with traditional French cooking and fine wines. It is a part of him that he will always cherish.

www.ingramcontent.com/pod-product-compliance
Lightning Source LLC
Chambersburg PA
CBHW071730150726
47998CB00005B/1581